# MLA Handbook

## EIGHTH EDITION

The Modern Language Association of America
New York 2016

The *MLA Handbook*, published by the Modern Language Association of America, provides the most accurate and complete instructions on MLA documentation style. For additional resources and updates, go to style.mla.org.



Library of Congress Cataloging-in-Publication Data

Name: Modern Language Association of America.
Title: MLA Handbook / Association of America, Modern Language.
Description: Eighth edition. | New York : The Modern Language Association of America, [2016] | Previous title: MLA Handbook for writers of research papers. | Includes bibliographical references and index.
Identifiers: LCCN 2015040898 (print) | LCCN 2015047757 (e-book) | ISBN 9781603292627 (pbk. : alk. paper) | ISBN 9781603292641 (EPUB) | ISBN 9781603292658 (Kindle)
Subjects: LCSH: Report writing—Handbooks, manuals, etc. | Research—Handbooks, manuals, etc.
Classification: LCC LB2369 .G53 2016 (print) | LCC LB2369 (e-book) | DDC 808.02/7—dc23
LC record available at http://lccn.loc.gov/2015040898

Fifth printing 2018

To purchase this and other MLA publications, visit www.mla.org/bookstore. For orders outside the United States, please contact the Eurospan Group (eurospan@turpin-distribution.com).

Published by The Modern Language Association of America
85 Broad Street, suite 500
New York, New York 10004-2434

# Contents

**Foreword by Rosemary G. Feal vii**

**Preface by Kathleen Fitzpatrick ix**

**Part 1**
**Principles of MLA Style**

Introduction 3

Why Document Sources? 5

Plagiarism and Academic Dishonesty 6

Think: Evaluating Your Sources 10

Select: Gathering Information about Your Sources 13

Organize: Creating Your Documentation 19

- The List of Works Cited 20
  - The Core Elements 20
    - Author 21
    - Title of Source 25
    - Title of Container 30
    - Other Contributors 37
    - Version 38
    - Number 39
    - Publisher 40
    - Publication Date 42
    - Location 46

Optional Elements 50
In-Text Citations 54

## Part 2
## Details of MLA Style

Introduction 61

1. The Mechanics of Scholarly Prose 61

1.1 Names of Persons 61
1.1.1 First and Subsequent Uses of Names 61
1.1.2 Titles of Authors 62
1.1.3 Names of Authors and Fictional Characters 62
1.1.4 Names in Languages Other Than English 63

1.2 Titles of Sources 67
1.2.1 Capitalization and Punctuation 67
1.2.2 Italics and Quotation Marks 68
1.2.3 Shortened Titles 70
1.2.4 Titles within Titles 71
1.2.5 Titles of Sources in Languages Other Than English 72

1.3 Quotations 75
1.3.1 Use and Accuracy of Quotations 75
1.3.2 Prose 75
1.3.3 Poetry 77
1.3.4 Drama 80
1.3.5 Ellipsis 80
1.3.6 Other Alterations of Quotations 86
1.3.7 Punctuation with Quotations 87
1.3.8 Translations of Quotations 90

1.4 Numbers 92
1.4.1 Use of Numerals or Words 92
1.4.2 Commas in Numbers 92
1.4.3 Inclusive Numbers 93
1.4.4 Roman Numerals 93

1.5 Dates and Times 94

1.6 Abbreviations 95
1.6.1 Months 95
1.6.2 Common Academic Abbreviations 96
1.6.3 Publishers' Names 97
1.6.4 Titles of Works 97
2. Works Cited 102
2.1 Names of Authors 102
2.1.1 Variant Forms 102
2.1.2 Titles and Suffixes 103
2.1.3 Corporate Authors 104
2.2 Titles 105
2.2.1 Introduction, Preface, Foreword, or Afterword 106
2.2.2 Translations of Titles 106
2.3 Versions 107
2.4 Publisher 107
2.5 Locational Elements 110
2.5.1 Plus Sign with Page Number 110
2.5.2 URLs and DOIs 110
2.6 Punctuation in the Works-Cited List 110
2.6.1 Square Brackets 111
2.6.2 Forward Slash 111
2.7 Formatting and Ordering the Works-Cited List 111
2.7.1 Letter-by-Letter Alphabetization 112
2.7.2 Multiple Works by One Author 113
2.7.3 Multiple Works by Coauthors 114
2.7.4 Alphabetizing by Title 115
2.7.5 Cross-References 115
3. In-Text Citations 116
3.1 Author 116
3.1.1 Coauthors 116
3.1.2 Corporate Author 117
3.2 Title 117

3.2.1 Abbreviating Titles of Sources 117
3.2.2 Descriptive Terms in Place of Titles 118
3.3 Numbers in In-Text Citations 119
3.3.1 Style of Numerals 119
3.3.2 Numbers in Works Available in Multiple Editions 120
3.3.3 Other Citations Not Involving Page Numbers 123
3.4 Indirect Sources 124
3.5 Repeated Use of Sources 124
3.6 Punctuation in the In-Text Citation 126
4. Citations in Forms Other Than Print 127
**Practice Template 129**
**Index 131**

# Foreword

In 1883 a small group of distinguished scholars came together with a radical idea: that modern languages deserved the same respect in higher education as classical languages (Greek and Latin). They decided to form an organization that would advocate language study, research, and the evolution of scholarship. The organization they founded is the Modern Language Association. Today the MLA has over 25,000 members in the United States, in Canada, and around the world.

Since its founding, the organization has been committed to sharing ideas and research. Its notable publications include the *MLA International Bibliography*, a major resource for researchers in literature and language, and *PMLA*, one of the most respected journals of literary studies. But the publication best known to the wider public is surely the *MLA Handbook*, which has served as the "style bible" for generations of students. Like the association, it has evolved in response to changing needs over the years.

I am especially pleased to present the eighth edition of the *MLA Handbook*, because it embodies so many of the values that define the association: a commitment to sharing ideas, a belief in scholarship as the work of a broad community, and a recognition that, while methods and media may change, basic principles of research stay the same. Designed in consultation with students, teachers, and researchers, this edition gives users more freedom to create references to fit their audiences. The recommendations continue to represent the consensus of teachers and scholars but offer a greater flexibility that will better accommodate new media and new ways of doing research.

We release new editions of the *MLA Handbook* when developments in scholarly research and writing call for changes in MLA style. The eighth edition brings one of our greatest shifts ever and, we believe, will serve the needs of students, teachers, and scholars today and in coming years. As always, we will be happy to hear from readers of this edition so that we can improve future iterations of MLA style.

Rosemary G. Feal
Executive Director
Modern Language Association

# Preface

"Has an element of fetishism perhaps crept into what was once a necessary academic practice?" So asks the writer and translator Tim Parks as he expresses his frustration with the process of creating the source documentation to be included in his forthcoming book—not least because he wonders whether the Internet has rendered that information superfluous. I am certain that many writers today experience similar frustration and raise similar doubts when detailing the sources with which they work. Given that this is the preface to the new edition of the authoritative guide to MLA documentation practice, you might expect that I intend to refute Parks's question. I do take issue with it, but for reasons perhaps different from the ones you might assume. The author is right to note that scholarly documentation has over decades acquired increasingly complex rules and formats, as well as to suggest that some of the information traditionally included in citations may be dispensed with today. He's not right, however, that documentation was "once" a necessity and is now obsolete thanks to search engines and full-text databases. If anything, the increasing use of such tools and resources by students and scholars makes the inclusion of a reliable data trail for future searchers even more important.

The problem, let me hasten to add, does not arise from the supposed ephemerality of digital tools and databases. Nor does this preface or the following guide assume that paper is secure and that bits, networks, and screens are fragile. The problem, rather, is the increasing mobility of texts. The sources with which we work are often discovered in locations and formats different from those in which they were originally published, and we have no way of knowing today where those sources might end up tomorrow. Moreover, for all the wonders of Internet search engines, they cannot be counted on to yield the right references every time we issue a query, because the algorithms used by search engines often base the presentation of results on popularity or even sponsorship. If a quotation in a text lacks documentation, an Internet search may be the only way to locate the original source, but the search may yield irrelevant works that contain the same passage. And even if the search locates a copy of the source, readers can't be certain that it's a faithful copy and thus that they'll see the same thing in it that the author who quoted from the original saw. All this is to say that the reasons for documenting sources in academic writing extend beyond simply giving a generic credit to the work from which a quotation or other borrowing was derived. Documentation is the means through which scholarly conversations are recorded, and the specifics of those conversations matter.

This edition of the *MLA Handbook* works to foreground those conversations among authors and between writer and reader. Before we get to the goals and strategies of the volume you hold in your hands (or see on your screen or encounter in some way I haven't yet imagined), it's worth rehearsing the history of documentation practices and, in particular, the development of MLA style.

In 1951 William Riley Parker, then the executive director of the Modern Language Association, published *The MLA Style Sheet*, a thirty-one-page pamphlet that sought to be a "more or less official" guide to the writing conventions then in use at more than eighty scholarly journals. The call issued by the style sheet for consistency in academic expression was tempered by an acknowledgment that "many problems of style cannot be reduced to rules even if everyone could agree" (3). The release of this document expanded the consensus, however; more journal and book publishers adopted

MLA style for their publications, and numerous universities required it for student papers.

In addition to recommendations on the preparation of documents ("In general, TYPE your manuscript to meet the very practical needs of your editor and printer" [4]) and on conventional aspects of writing, including spelling and the use of quotations and numerals, *The MLA Style Sheet* proposed a coherent system for documenting sources. That system relied primarily on footnotes, examples of which were included in the style sheet and supported by a long accompanying list of abbreviations designed to keep the footnotes brief.

A revised and expanded edition of *The MLA Style Sheet* was published in 1970, updating MLA style to reduce the use of roman numerals and to add publishers' names to bibliographic citations. It maintained a focus on the needs of scholars who intended to publish the results of their research. In 1977 the first edition of the *MLA Handbook* gave its attention to the needs of students. This 163-page guide adopted the expressly pedagogical aim of helping student writers of research papers understand and implement the conventions of academic prose. The second edition of the handbook (221 pages) was released in 1984 and was accompanied the following year by the first edition of the *MLA Style Manual*, which took established scholars and graduate students as its audience, sharpening the handbook's focus on undergraduate writing.

This history suggests that while there is a temptation to think of MLA style as an unchanging monolith—a singular way of doing things—the style has in fact evolved, and it has at moments undergone radical transformation (such as the shift, in 1984, from footnotes to the list of works cited and corresponding in-text references). Modifications came about in response to developments in literary studies, as well as to the changing needs of students. Over the years, however, the handbook gained what some felt was a forbidding level of detail (the seventh edition was 292 pages long). It gradually became a reference work, which users consulted at need, rather than a guide that taught the principles underlying documentation.

In publishing the eighth edition of the *MLA Handbook*, we aim to better meet the needs of students today by offering a quick but thorough introduction to the hows and whys of using sources in academic writing. We hope that this reorientation will convey what we believe to be the most important aspect of academic writing: its engagement with the reader, which obligates the author to ensure that the reader has all the information necessary to understand the text at hand without being distracted from it by the citations.

In a citation-by-citation comparison, this new version of MLA style may appear to differ only slightly from established practice, but the approach we take in this volume foregrounds principles. While the seventh edition of the *MLA Handbook* described the style it presented as "flexible" and "modular," providing "several sequences of elements that can be combined to form entries" (129), the style was nonetheless based on defining a citation format for each kind of source. Thus, until now the handbook presented separate rules for citing a book, a journal article, a newspaper article, a personal letter, and all the rest in the ever-expanding range of sources that writers use in their work. As a result, with the emergence of each new media platform would come a new query: How do you cite a *YouTube* video? a blog post? a tweet?

With the eighth edition, we shift our focus from a prescriptive list of formats to the overarching purpose of source documentation: enabling readers to participate fully in the conversations between writers and their sources. Such participation requires the presentation of reliable information in a clear, consistent structure, but we believe that if we concentrate on the principles undergirding MLA style and on the ways they can be applied in a broad range of cases, we can craft a truly flexible documentation practice that will continue to serve writers well in a changing environment. Moreover, this edition recognizes that different kinds of scholarly conversations require different kinds of documentation and thus that the application of principles might vary according to context. It therefore focuses on the writer's decision making. It offers a new approach to thinking about MLA style, one centered not on a source's publication format but rather on the elements common to most sources and on the means of flexibly combining those elements to create appropriate documentation for any source.

Change is perhaps the one constant of contemporary academic life. The first edition of the *MLA Style Manual* noted "numerous innovations affecting scholarly publication," including "the widespread use of word processors" (Achtert and Gibaldi vii), and change has only accelerated in recent years, making flexibility and openness increasingly important. In the eighth edition, we therefore embrace the fact that student research and writing today take many forms other than the research paper, and so we begin what we expect to be an ongoing exploration of the best means of documenting sources in new modes of academic writing. Just as research sources have become mobile, so too have the works that a researcher creates: they appear in print but are also projected on screens and displayed on reading devices. The citations a researcher today produces are appended to traditional, linear texts, but they are also attached to weblike texts and even to projects that aren't texts at all. If this edition of the *MLA Handbook* lets go of some of what Parks called an "element of fetishism" in scholarly documentation practices, it nonetheless argues that documentation remains a core academic principle, one that can be adapted to new circumstances.

Developing this edition and the new understanding of MLA style that it conveys required the energy and attention of many scholars, instructors, editors, and librarians. The edition builds on the work done before me, including the important contributions of William Riley Parker, Walter S. Achtert, Joseph Gibaldi, and David G. Nicholls. Though I was primarily responsible for writing the text that follows, I could not have managed it without the efforts and wisdom of the MLA staff members who work most closely with MLA style day in and day out: Angela Gibson, Judy Goulding, James Hatch, Margit Longbrake, Sara Pastel, and Eric Wirth, who together rethought the principles of MLA style for the twenty-first century. We consulted along the way with a wide range of MLA members, including members of the Committee on Information Technology, the Publications Committee, and the Executive Council. Many experts read early drafts of the manuscript; among this group we particularly thank Andi Adkins-Pogue, Carolyn Ayers, Rebecca Babcock, Delores Carlito, Brooke Carlson, Kelly Diamond, Keri Donovan, Michael Elam, Lindsay Hansen, Nicki Lerczak, Sara Marcus, Debra Ryals, Thomas Smith, Jeanne Swedo, Araceli Tinajero, and Belinda Wheeler.

Transforming the manuscript into a finished publication was also the work of many hands. The design, typesetting, electronic processing, and printing were handled by David F. Cope, Tom Lewek, Pamela Roller, Laurie Russell, and Patrice Sheridan, under the supervision of Judith Altreuter.

This edition of the *MLA Handbook* is accompanied by online resources (see style.mla.org). We hope that you will explore these resources and let us know what else you would find useful.

Finally, thanks are due to Rosemary G. Feal, the executive director of the MLA, and to the members of the MLA Executive Council for their vision and leadership in shaping the future of scholarly communication in the humanities.

Kathleen Fitzpatrick
Associate Executive Director and
Director of Scholarly Communication
Modern Language Association

## Works Cited

Achtert, Walter S., and Joseph Gibaldi. *The MLA Style Manual*. MLA, 1985.

*MLA Handbook for Writers of Research Papers*. 7th ed., MLA, 2009.

Parker, William Riley. *The MLA Style Sheet*. 1951. Rev. ed., MLA, 1962.

Parks, Tim. "References, Please." *NYR Daily*, New York Review of Books, 13 Sept. 2014, www.nybooks.com/blogs/nyrblog/2014/sep/13/references-please/.

# PART 1

# Principles of MLA Style

# Introduction

In today's world, forms of communication proliferate, and publications migrate readily from one medium to another. An article published in a print journal may be discovered and read online, through one of many databases; an episode of a television series may be watched through a service like *Hulu*; a blog post may be republished as a book chapter. Even as we developed this edition of the *MLA Handbook*, new publication formats and platforms emerged.

As a result, now more than ever we need a system for documenting sources that begins with a few principles rather than a long list of rules. Rules remain important, and we will get to them in due course, but in this section we emphasize commonsense guidelines aimed at helping writers at various levels conduct research and provide their audiences with useful information about their sources.

Your use of MLA style should be guided by these principles:

### *Cite simple traits shared by most works.*

In previous editions of the *MLA Handbook*, an entry in the works-cited list was based on the source's publication format (e.g., book, film, magazine article, Web publication). The writer first determined the format of the source and then collected the publication facts associated with the format. A consequence of that approach was that works in a new medium could not be documented until the MLA created instructions for it. This edition, by contrast, is not centered on publication formats. It deals instead with facts common to most works—author, title, and so on. The writer examines the source and records its visible features, attending to the work itself and a set of universal guidelines. A work in a new medium thus can be documented without new instructions.

***Remember that there is often more than one correct way to document a source.***

Different situations call for different solutions. A writer whose primary purpose is to give credit for borrowed material may need to provide less information than a writer who is examining the distinguishing features of particular editions (or even specific copies) of source texts. Similarly, scholars working in specialized fields may need to cite details about their sources that other scholars making more general use of the same resources do not.

***Make your documentation useful to readers.***

Good writers understand why they create citations. The reasons include demonstrating the thoroughness of the writer's research, giving credit to original sources, and ensuring that readers can find the sources consulted in order to draw their own conclusions about the writer's argument. Writers achieve the goals of documentation by providing sufficient information in a comprehensible, consistent structure.

This edition of the *MLA Handbook* is designed to help writers *think* about the sources they are documenting, *select* the information about the sources that is appropriate to the project they are creating, and *organize* it logically and without complication. Armed with a few rules and an understanding of the basic principles, a writer can generate useful documentation of any work, in any publication format.

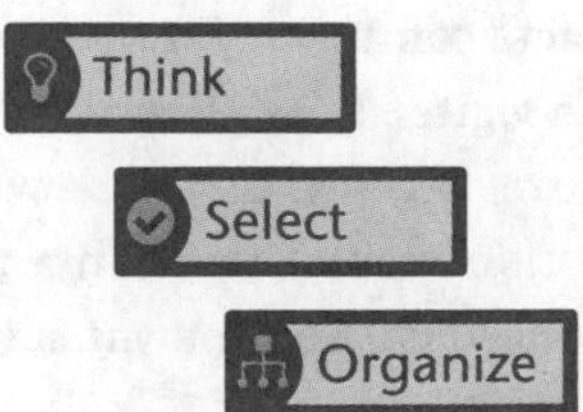

# Why Document Sources?

Documenting sources is an aspect of writing common to all academic fields. Across the natural sciences, the social sciences, and the humanities, authors use standard techniques to refer to the works that influenced or otherwise contributed to their research. Why?

Academic writing is at its root a conversation among scholars about a topic or question. Scholars write for their peers, communicating the results of their research through books, journal articles, and other forms of published work. In the course of a project, they seek out relevant publications, to learn from and build on earlier research. Through their own published work, they incorporate, modify, respond to, and refute previous publications.

Given the importance of this conversation to research, authors must have comprehensible, verifiable means of referring to one another's work. Such references enable them to give credit to the precursors whose ideas they borrow, build on, or contradict and allow future researchers interested in the history of the conversation to trace it back to its beginning. The references are formatted in a standard way so that they can be quickly understood and used by all, like a common language.

Students are called on to learn documentation styles in a range of courses throughout their education, but not because it is expected that all students will take up such research practices in their professional lives. Rather, learning the conventions of a form of writing—those of the research essay, for instance—prepares the student to write not just in that form but in other ones as well.

Learning a documentation style, in other words, prepares a writer to be on the lookout for the conventions to which every professional field expects its members to adhere in their writing. Legal documents must refer to prior legal documents in a standard way to be acceptable in the legal profession. Reports on scientific research must refer to earlier research in the fashion expected in a particular scientific field. Business documents point to published information and use a language and format that are accepted in business. Journalists similarly obey conventions for identifying their sources, structuring their stories, and so on. The conventions differ from one profession to another, but their purpose is the same.

Learning good documentation practices is also a key component of academic integrity. However, avoiding charges of plagiarism is not the only reason that a student should learn to document sources. The proper use of a field's preferred documentation style is a sign of competence in a writer. Among other benefits, it shows that the writer knows the importance of giving credit where credit is due. It therefore helps the writer become part of a community of scholars and assures readers that the writer's work can be trusted.

## Plagiarism and Academic Dishonesty

You may have heard or read about cases in which a politician, a journalist, or another public figure was accused of plagiarism. No doubt you have also had classroom conversations about plagiarism and academic dishonesty. Your school may have an honor code that addresses academic dishonesty; it almost certainly has disciplinary procedures meant to address cases of plagiarism. But you may nonetheless find yourself with questions: What is plagiarism? What makes it a serious offense? What does it look like? And how can scrupulous research and documentation practices help you avoid it?

### *What Is Plagiarism?*

*Merriam-Webster's Collegiate Dictionary* defines plagiarizing as committing "literary theft." Plagiarism is presenting another person's ideas, information, expressions, or entire work as one's own. It is thus a kind of fraud: deceiving others to gain something of value. While plagiarism only sometimes has legal repercussions (e.g., when it involves copyright infringement—violating an author's exclusive legal right to publication), it is always a serious moral and ethical offense.

### *What Makes Plagiarism a Serious Offense?*

Plagiarists are seen not only as dishonest but also as incompetent, incapable of doing research and expressing original thoughts. When professional writers are exposed as plagiarists, they are likely to lose their jobs and are certain to suffer public embarrassment, diminished prestige, and loss of future credibility. The same is true of other professionals who write in connection with their jobs, even when they are not writing for publication. The charge of plagiarism is serious because it calls into question everything about the writer's work: if *this* piece of writing is misrepresented as being original, how can a reader trust any work by the writer? One instance of plagiarism can cast a shadow across an entire career.

Schools consider plagiarism a grave matter for the same reason. If a student fails to give credit for the work of others in one project, how can a teacher trust any of the student's work? Plagiarism undermines the relationship between teachers and students, turning teachers into detectives instead of mentors, fostering suspicion instead of trust, and making it difficult for learning to take place. Students who plagiarize deprive themselves of the knowledge they would have gained if they had done their own writing. Plagiarism also can undermine public trust in educational institutions, if students are routinely allowed to pass courses and receive diplomas without doing the required work.

### *What Does Plagiarism Look Like?*

Plagiarism can take a number of forms, including buying papers from a service on the Internet, reusing work done by another student, and copying text from published sources without giving credit to those who produced the sources. All forms of plagiarism have in common the misrepresentation of work not done by the writer as the writer's own. (And, yes, that includes work you pay for: while celebrities may put their names on work by ghostwriters, students may not.)

Even borrowing just a few words from an author without clearly indicating that you did so constitutes plagiarism. Moreover, you can plagiarize unintentionally; in hastily taken notes, it is easy to mistake a phrase copied from a source as your original thought and then to use it without crediting the source.

Imagine, for example, that you read the following passage in the course of your research (from Michael Agar's book *Language Shock*):

> Everyone uses the word *language* and everybody these days talks about *culture*. . . . "Languaculture" is a reminder, I hope, of the *necessary* connection between its two parts. . . .

If you wrote the following sentence, it would constitute plagiarism:

> At the intersection of language and culture lies a concept that we might call "languaculture."

Is it possible to plagiarize yourself? Yes, it is. If you reuse ideas or phrases that you used in prior work and do not cite the prior work, you have plagiarized. Many academic honesty policies prohibit the reuse of one's prior work, even with a citation. If you want to reuse your work, consult with your instructor.

This sentence borrows a word from Agar's work without giving credit for it. Placing the term in quotation marks is insufficient. If you use the term, you must give credit to its source:

> At the intersection of language and culture lies a concept that Michael Agar has called "languaculture" (60).

In this version, a reference to the original author and a parenthetical citation indicate the source of the term; a corresponding entry in your list of works cited will give your reader full information about the source.

It's important to note that you need not copy an author's words to be guilty of plagiarism; if you paraphrase someone's ideas or arguments without giving credit for their origin, you have committed plagiarism. Imagine that you read the following passage (from Walter A. McDougall's *Promised Land, Crusader State: The American Encounter with the World since 1776*):

> American Exceptionalism as our founders conceived it was defined by what America *was*, at home. Foreign policy existed to defend, not define, what America was.

If you write the following sentence, you have plagiarized, even though you changed some of the wording:

> For the founding fathers America's exceptionalism was based on the country's domestic identity, which foreign policy did not shape but merely guarded.

In this sentence, you have borrowed an author's ideas without acknowledgment. You may use the ideas, however, if you properly give credit to your source:

> As Walter A. McDougall argues, for the founding fathers America's exceptionalism was based on the country's domestic identity, which foreign policy did not shape but merely guarded (37).

In this revised sentence, which includes an in-text citation and clearly gives credit to McDougall as the source of the idea, there is no plagiarism.

### *How Can You Avoid Plagiarism?*

Avoiding plagiarism begins with being scrupulous in your research and note-taking. Keep a complete and thorough list of all the sources that you discover during your research and wish to use, linking each source to the information you glean from it, so that you can double-check that your work acknowledges it. Take care in your notes to distinguish between what is not yours and what is yours, identifying ideas and phrases copied from sources you consult, summaries of your sources, and your own original ideas. As you write, carefully identify all borrowed material, including quoted words and phrases, paraphrased ideas, summarized arguments, and facts and other information.

Most important is that you check with your instructor if you are unsure about the way that you are using a particular source.

### *Does Absence of Documentation Indicate Plagiarism?*

Documentation is not required for every type of borrowed material. Information and ideas that are common knowledge among your readers need not be documented. Common knowledge includes information widely available in reference works, such as basic biographical facts about prominent persons and the dates and circumstances of major historical events. When the facts are in dispute, however, or when your readers may want more information about your topic, it is good practice to document the material you borrow.

The rest of this section will guide you through the steps involved in giving credit for others' work. Documentation begins well before you put together your list of works cited. Sound academic use of sources starts with evaluating them and selecting the appropriate information from them.

## Think EVALUATING YOUR SOURCES

In writing a research paper, putting together a presentation, creating an online project, or doing other kinds of academic work, you will gather sources that inform, support, or otherwise help you shape your argument. The gathering of sources used to be more arduous than it is today: researchers had to spend hours in the library, tracking down printed indexes and bibliographies, locating the works uncovered, and then obtaining physical copies of the works. One part of this process used to be easier, however: a researcher could assume that the works found were reliable, since they were discovered through professionally compiled indexes and in professionally curated collections.

Today the Internet, with its many publications, databases, archives, and search engines, has accelerated the process of finding and retrieving sources—but at the same time it has complicated the researcher's assessment of their reliability. The amount and variety of information available have grown exponentially, but the origins of that information are too often unclear.

The first step, therefore, in gathering sources for your academic work is to evaluate them, asking yourself questions such as these:

**Who** is the author of the source? Is the author qualified to address the subject? Does the author draw on appropriate research and make a logical argument? Do you perceive bias or the possibility of it in the author's relation to the subject matter?

**What** is the source? Does it have a title, and does that title tell you anything about it? If it lacks a title, how would you describe it? Is it a primary source, such as an original document, creative work, or artifact, or a secondary source, which reports on or analyzes primary sources? If it is an edition, is it authoritative? Does the source document its own sources in a trustworthy manner?

**How** was the source produced? Does it have a recognized publisher or sponsoring organization? Was it subjected to a process of vetting, such as peer review, through which authorities in the field assessed its quality?

*Google* and *Wikipedia* are reasonable places to begin your research but not good places to end it. Follow up on the sources that *Wikipedia* entries cite. (Be sure to read the pages accompanying a *Wikipedia* entry, which give its history and the editors' discussions about it, since that information shows how the entry evolved and where the controversy in your subject lies.)

**Where** did you find the source? Was it cited in an authoritative work? Was it among the results of a search you conducted through a scholarly database (such as the *MLA International Bibliography*) or a library's resources? Did you discover it through a commercial search engine that may weight results by popularity or even payment?

**When** was the source published? Could its information have been supplemented or replaced by more recent work?

These are only a few of the questions that you might consider as you evaluate the sources you use in your work. Both your judgment and your awareness of your readers' expectations are crucial at this stage.

It is important to understand that research is a cyclic process. Scholars rarely find all the sources they need in a single search. You should expect to search, evaluate the sources you find, refocus or otherwise revise your searching strategy, and begin again.

As you do your research, keep complete, well-organized records that allow you to retrace your footsteps, since you may need to return to a source for more information. Keeping good notes will also simplify the task of documenting your sources. Digital reference managers can be helpful to this end, but they have limitations. They may overlook key information, capture the wrong information, or generate citations with improper formatting. You should understand how to create your own documentation even if you use a citation generator, so that you can correct the output and can produce it yourself if the citation generator is not available.

After gathering sources, evaluating them, and winnowing out those unsuitable for your research, you will record information about the ones you plan to consult. This information is the basis of your documentation.

Select

# Gathering Information about Your Sources

The source documentation in your finished project will be built from information you collect as you discover and read useful works. As you evaluated your sources, you asked yourself the following questions:

**Who** is the author of the source?
**What** is the title of the source?
**How** was the source published?
**Where** did you find the source?
**When** was the source published?

Each of these elements—author, title, publisher, location, publication date—has a place in your documentation, so keep track of them carefully. Be sure that you select the correct information about your sources. Examine the work itself for the facts about its publication. Do not rely on a listing found elsewhere, whether on the Web, in a library catalog, or in a reference book, because it may be erroneous or incomplete.

Facts missing from source *see sec. 2.6.1*

In general, you should look in the places where the source's publisher, editor, or author gives credit for or describes its production. The examples on pages 14–18 show where you can find publication facts about works in various media. We'll go into more detail about what information you need and what you do with it as we discuss organizing your documentation.

# Finding Facts about Publications

First consult the title page, not the cover or the top of a page.

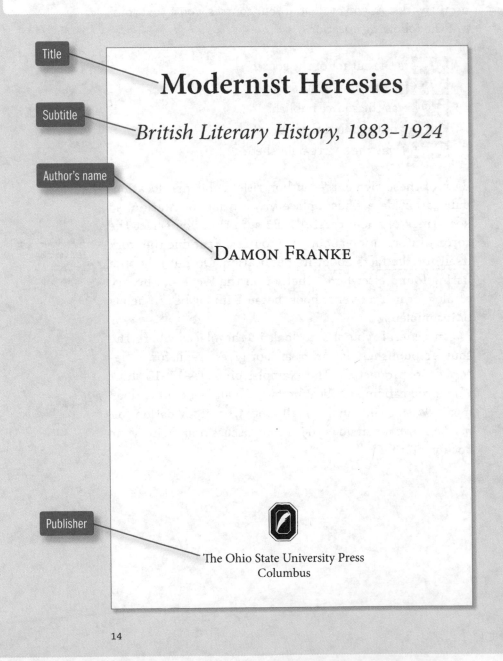

Title — **Modernist Heresies**

Subtitle — *British Literary History, 1883–1924*

Author's name — DAMON FRANKE

Publisher — The Ohio State University Press
Columbus

If the title page of a book lacks needed information, such as the date of publication, consult the book's copyright page (usually the reverse of the title page).

Date of publication

Copyright © 2008 by The Ohio State University.
All rights reserved.

Library of Congress Cataloging-in-Publication Data
Franke, Damon, 1968–
Modernist heresies : British literary history, 1883–1924 / Damon Franke.
p. cm.
Includes bibliographical references and index.
ISBN-13: 978–0–8142–1074–1 (cloth : alk. paper)
ISBN-13: 978–0–8142–9151–1 (CD-ROM)
1. Modernism (Literature)—Great Britain. 2. English literature—20th century—History and criticism. 3. English literature—19th century—History and criticism. 4. Religion and literature—Great Britain—History—20th century. 5. Religion and literature—Great Britain—History—19th century. 6. Great Britain—Intellectual life—20th century. 7. Great Britain—Intellectual life—19th century. 8. Heretics, Christian—Great Britain—History. 9. Heresies, Christian, in literature. 10. Paganism in literature. I. Title.
PR478.M6F73 2008
820.9'112—dc22

## Story, Poem, or Article in a Book or in a Periodical

Consult the first page of the text for the author and title of the work. The publication facts about an issue of a periodical (journal, magazine, newspaper) are usually found on the cover, on a title page, or near the table of contents.

Journal title

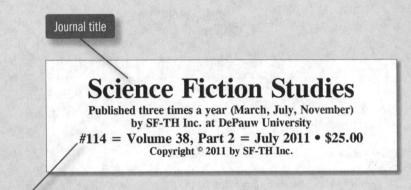

**Science Fiction Studies**

**Published three times a year (March, July, November)**
**by SF-TH Inc. at DePauw University**
**#114 = Volume 38, Part 2 = July 2011 • $25.00**
**Copyright © 2011 by SF-TH Inc.**

Publication facts about the issue

Author's name

NINETEENTH-CENTURY SF IN SPAIN 253

**Geraldine Lawless**

**Unknown Futures: Nineteenth-Century Science Fiction in Spain**

Title of article

In her *SFS* review of Stelio Cro's edition of the previously unpublished early Spanish utopia called *Sinapia*, Sylvia Winter expressed her excitement at the [...]ry of the work, saying "*Sinapia* may well constitute, up to this point, the only literary utopia written from the perspective of what has been described as the semi-peripheral areas of the modern world system" (100). With the qualification "up to this point," Winter avoids generalizations about the non-existence of literary utopias in certain parts of the globe. Such careful wording does not always characterize literary histories. Her cautious approach raises an important question about the literary histories of Spain and about the history of

## Work on the Web

Web sources may require you to look in more than one place for the information you need. The Web page on which you found the work will have some facts. Along with other information there, copy the URL of the page into your notes. If the page lacks needed information, such as the name of the site's publisher, look for a link that reads "About this site" or has similar wording.

Some Web sites specify works-cited-list entries for their contents. Such examples might provide you with useful information about the site but will not necessarily conform to the system in this handbook, even if they are labeled "MLA style."

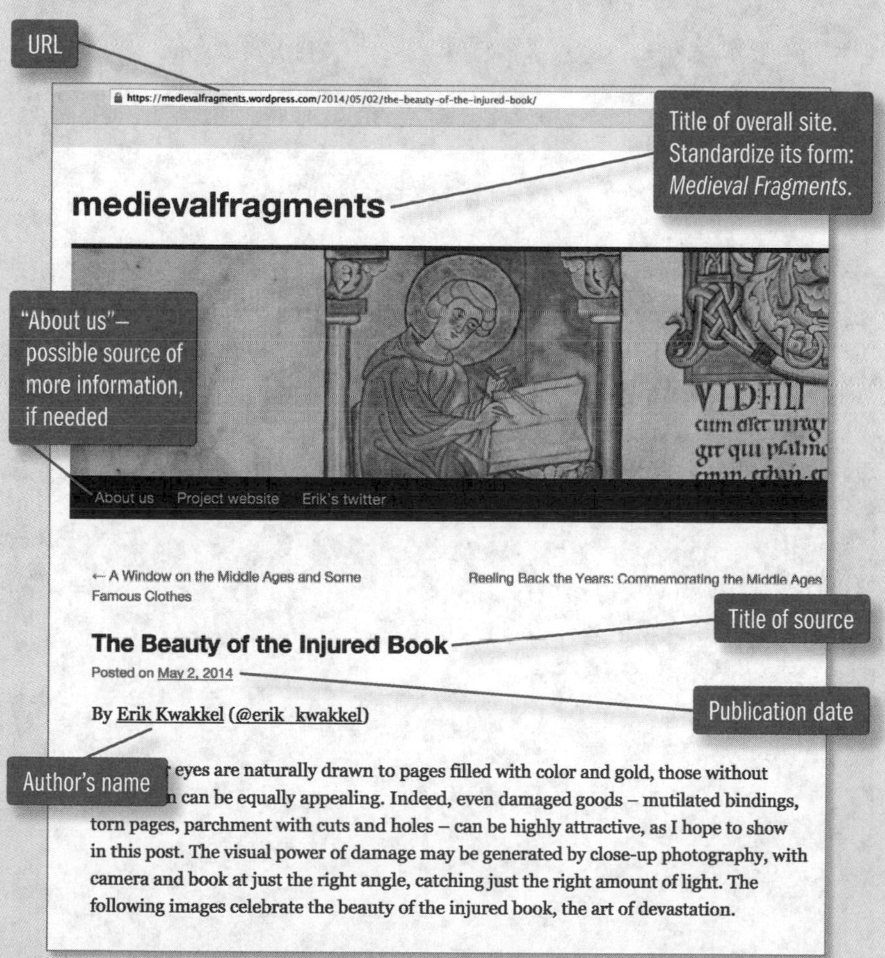

## Work in Film, Video, or Television

A work in a medium like film, video, or television usually contains credits that supply facts needed for documentation.

If credits are lacking in the work and you viewed it on a DVD or other disc, you may find the missing information on the disc's packaging.

## Organize CREATING YOUR DOCUMENTATION

Once you've evaluated the sources you used in your research and gathered the relevant information about them, it's time to organize the information into entries in the works-cited list and create in-text citations. The purpose of any documentation style is to allow authors to guide their readers quickly and unobtrusively to the source of a quotation, a paraphrased idea, a piece of information, or another kind of borrowed material used in the development of an argument or idea. A citation should provide a road map leading to the original source while interrupting the reader's engagement with the text as little as possible.

Minimizing interruptions is a goal in many kinds of writing. If readers are to be engaged and involved in an idea or issue, the reading process should be smooth and unimpeded. Every time readers have to stop and figure something out—whether it's deciphering the intent of stray punctuation, puzzling over a misspelled or misused word, stumbling over an incorrectly structured citation, or wondering about a reference to a source not in the works-cited list—they are distracted from the argument at hand, and their distraction hinders engagement with the author's point. If a piece of writing is as clear and error-free as possible and if its documentation is trustworthy, readers will remain focused on the ideas.

To satisfy the two requirements of completeness and brevity, documentation in MLA style has two parts. The first part is a detailed entry in a list of works cited; the second is a citation in the text, a minimal reference that directs the reader to the entry. We'll discuss each of these in turn.

## The List of Works Cited

The list titled "Works Cited" identifies the sources you borrow from—and therefore cite—in the body of your research project. Works that you consult during your research but do not borrow from are not included (if you want to document them as well and your instructor approves their inclusion, give the list a broader title, such as "Works Consulted"). Each entry in the list of works cited is made up of core elements given in a specific order, and there are optional elements that may be included when the situation warrants.

### The Core Elements

The core elements of any entry in the works-cited list are given below in the order in which they should appear. An element should be omitted from the entry if it's not relevant to the work being documented. Each element is followed by the punctuation mark shown unless it is the final element, which should end with a period.

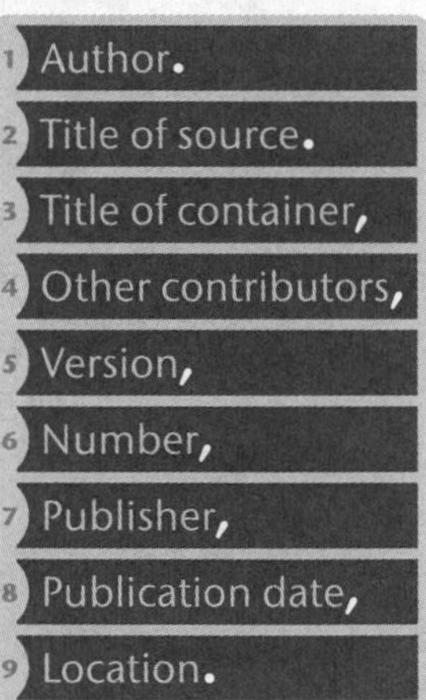

1 Author.
2 Title of source.
3 Title of container,
4 Other contributors,
5 Version,
6 Number,
7 Publisher,
8 Publication date,
9 Location.


In what follows, we'll explain each of these elements, how you'll find them, and how they might differ from one medium to another.

## 1 Author.

The author's name is usually prominently displayed in a work, often near the title (see fig. 1). Begin the entry with the author's last name, followed by a comma and the rest of the name, as presented in the work. End this element with a period (unless a period that is part of the author's name already appears at the end).

More about authors' names *see sec. 2.1*

Multiple works by one author *see sec. 2.7.2*

Baron, Naomi S. "Redefining Reading: The Impact of Digital Communication Media." *PMLA*, vol. 128, no. 1, Jan. 2013, pp. 193-200.

Jacobs, Alan. *The Pleasures of Reading in an Age of Distraction.* Oxford UP, 2011.

Kincaid, Jamaica. "In History." *Callaloo*, vol. 24, no. 2, Spring 2001, pp. 620-26.

When a source has **two authors**, include them in the order in which they are presented in the work (see fig. 2). Reverse the first of the names as just described, follow it with a comma and *and*, and give the second name in normal order.

Multiple works by coauthors *see sec. 2.7.3*

Dorris, Michael, and Louise Erdrich. *The Crown of Columbus.* HarperCollins Publishers, 1999.

**IN HISTORY**

*by Jamaica Kincaid*

What to call the thing that happened to me and all who look like me?
Should I call it history?
If so, what should history mean to someone like me?

Author's name

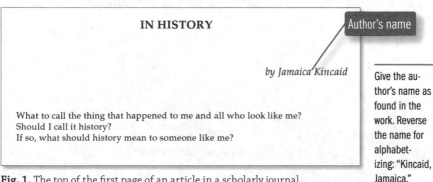

**Fig. 1.** The top of the first page of an article in a scholarly journal.

Give the author's name as found in the work. Reverse the name for alphabetizing: "Kincaid, Jamaica."

When a source has **three or more authors**, reverse the first of the names as just described and follow it with a comma and *et al.* ("and others").

> Burdick, Anne, et al. *Digital_Humanities.* MIT P, 2012.

We use the term *author* loosely here: it refers to the person or group primarily responsible for producing the work or the aspect of the work that you focused on. If the role of that person or group was something other than

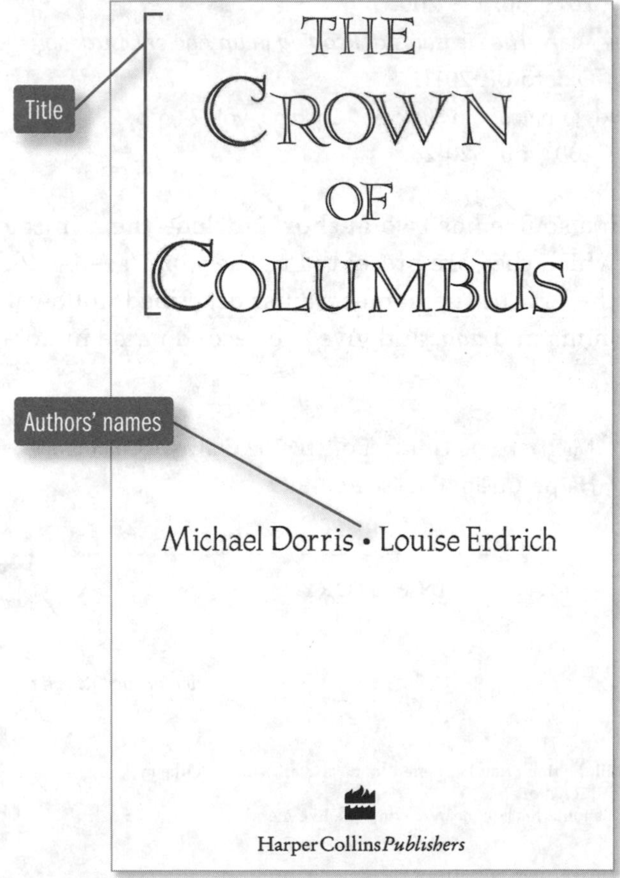

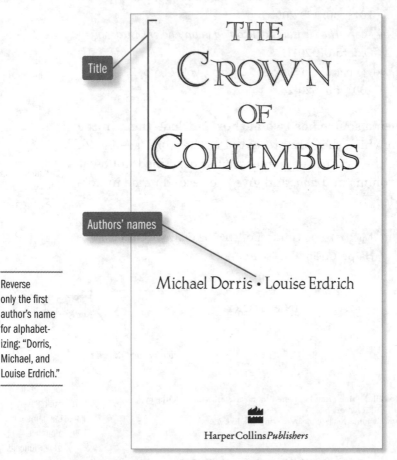

Reverse only the first author's name for alphabetizing: "Dorris, Michael, and Louise Erdrich."

**Fig. 2.** The title page of a book. Two authors are shown.

creating the work's main content, follow the name with a label that describes the role. For example, if the source is an edited volume of essays that you need to document as a whole, the "author" for your purposes is the person who assembled the volume—its **editor**. Since the editor did not create the main content, the name is followed by a descriptive label.

> Nunberg, Geoffrey, editor. *The Future of the Book.* U of California P, 1996.

A source with **two or more editors** requires combining the two methods just described (and making the descriptive label plural).

> Baron, Sabrina Alcorn, et al., editors. *Agent of Change: Print Culture Studies after Elizabeth L. Eisenstein.* U of Massachusetts P / Center for the Book, Library of Congress, 2007.
>
> Holland, Merlin, and Rupert Hart-Davis, editors. *The Complete Letters of Oscar Wilde.* Henry Holt, 2000.

When you discuss a source that was **translated from another language** and your focus is on the translation, treat the translator as the author.

> Pevear, Richard, and Larissa Volokhonsky, translators. *Crime and Punishment.* By Fyodor Dostoevsky, Vintage eBooks, 1993.
>
> Sullivan, Alan, and Timothy Murphy, translators. *Beowulf.* Edited by Sarah Anderson, Pearson, 2004.

If the name of the creator of the work's main content does not appear at the start of the entry (as in the example for *Crime and Punishment*, above), give that name, preceded by *By*, in the position of other contributors.

*see pp. 37–38*

Works in media such as **film and television** are usually produced by many people playing various roles. If your discussion of such a work focuses on the contribution of a particular person—say, the performance of an actor or the ideas of the screenwriter—begin the entry with his or her name, followed by a descriptive label.

Gellar, Sarah Michelle, performer. *Buffy the Vampire Slayer.* Mutant Enemy, 1997-2003.

Whedon, Joss, creator. *Buffy the Vampire Slayer.* Mutant Enemy, 1997-2003.

If you are writing about a film or television series without focusing on an individual's contribution, begin with the title. You can include information about the director and other key participants in the position of other contributors.

*Buffy the Vampire Slayer.* Created by Joss Whedon, performance by Sarah Michelle Gellar, Mutant Enemy, 1997-2003.

see sec. 2.1.1

**Pseudonyms**, including online usernames, are mostly given like regular author names.

see sec. 1.5

@persiankiwi. "We have report of large street battles in east & west of Tehran now - #Iranelection." *Twitter*, 23 June 2009, 11:15 a.m., twitter.com/persiankiwi/status/2298106072.

Stendhal. *The Red and the Black*. Translated by Roger Gard, Penguin Books, 2002.

Tribble, Ivan. "Bloggers Need Not Apply." *The Chronicle of Higher Education*, 8 July 2005, chronicle.com/article/Bloggers-Need-Not-Apply/45022.

When a work is published **without an author's name**, do not list the author as "Anonymous." Instead, skip the author element and begin the entry with the work's title.

*Beowulf.* Translated by Alan Sullivan and Timothy Murphy, edited by Sarah Anderson, Pearson, 2004.

Authors do not have to be individual persons. A work may be created by a **corporate author**—an institution, an association, a government agency, or another kind of organization.

see sec. 2.1.3

United Nations. *Consequences of Rapid Population Growth in Developing Countries.* Taylor and Francis, 1991.

When a work is published by an organization that is also its author, begin the entry with the title, skipping the author element, and list the organization only as publisher.

*Reading at Risk: A Survey of Literary Reading in America.* National Endowment for the Arts, June 2004.

## 2 Title of source.

More about titles see secs. 1.2, 2.2

After the author, the next element included in the entry in the works-cited list is the title of the source. The title is usually prominently displayed in the work, often near the author (see fig. 3).

Puig, Manuel. *Kiss of the Spider Woman.* Translated by Thomas Colchie, Vintage Books, 1991.

A subtitle is included after the main title (see fig. 4).

Joyce, Michael. *Othermindedness: The Emergence of Network Culture.* U of Michigan P, 2000.

Titles are given in the entry in full exactly as they are found in the source, except that capitalization and the punctuation between the main title and a subtitle are standardized.

see sec. 1.2.1

The appropriate formatting of titles helps your reader understand the nature of your sources on sight. A title is placed in quotation marks if the source is part of a larger work. A title is italicized (or underlined if italics are unavailable or undesirable) if the source is self-contained and

see sec. 1.2.2

independent. For example, a **book** is a whole unto itself, and so its title is set in italics.

> Jacobs, Alan. *The Pleasures of Reading in an Age of Distraction.* Oxford UP, 2011.

The same is true of a volume that is a **collection of essays, stories, or poems** by various authors.

> Baron, Sabrina Alcorn, et al., editors. *Agent of Change: Print Culture Studies after Elizabeth L. Eisenstein.* U of Massachusetts P / Center for the Book, Library of Congress, 2007.

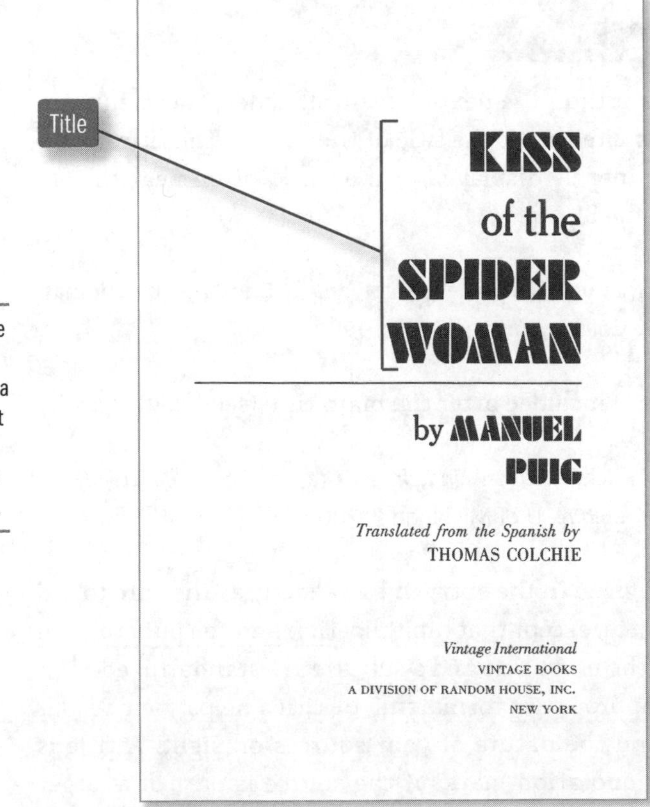


Standardize the capitalization when you copy a title in your text or works-cited list: *Kiss of the Spider Woman.*

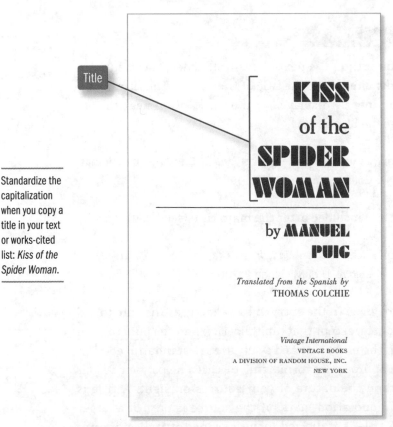

**Fig. 3.** The title page of a book.

The title of **an essay, a story, or a poem** in a collection, as a part of a larger whole, is placed in quotation marks.

> Dewar, James A., and Peng Hwa Ang. "The Cultural Consequences of Printing and the Internet." *Agent of Change: Print Culture Studies after Elizabeth L. Eisenstein*, edited by Sabrina Alcorn Baron et al., U of Massachusetts P / Center for the Book, Library of Congress, 2007, pp. 365-77.

When a work that is normally independent (such as a novel or play) appears in a collection (*Ten Plays*, below), the work's title remains in italics.

> Euripides. *The Trojan Women*. *Ten Plays*, translated by Paul Roche, New American Library, 1998, pp. 457-512.

The title of a **periodical** (journal, magazine, newspaper) is set in italics, and the title of an **article** in the periodical goes in quotation marks.

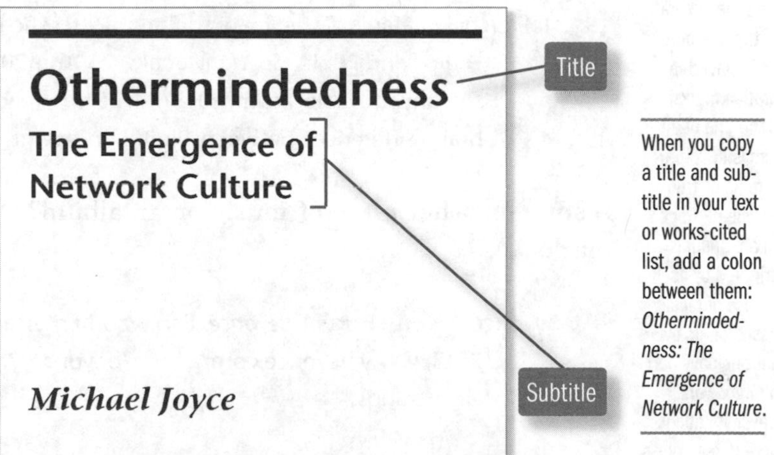


When you copy a title and subtitle in your text or works-cited list, add a colon between them: *Othermindedness: The Emergence of Network Culture*.

**Fig. 4.** Part of the title page of a book. The type design makes clear the distinction between the title and subtitle.

Goldman, Anne. "Questions of Transport: Reading Primo Levi Reading Dante." *The Georgia Review*, vol. 64, no. 1, 2010, pp. 69-88.

The rule applies across media forms. The title of a **television series**? Italics.

*Buffy the Vampire Slayer*. Created by Joss Whedon, performance by Sarah Michelle Gellar, Mutant Enemy, 1997-2003.

The title of an **episode** of a television series? Quotation marks.

"Hush." *Buffy the Vampire Slayer*, created by Joss Whedon, performance by Sarah Michelle Gellar, season 4, episode 10, Mutant Enemy, 1999.

A **Web site**? Italics.

Hollmichel, Stefanie. *So Many Books*. 2003-13, somanybooksblog.com.

A **posting or an article** at a Web site? Quotation marks.

Hollmichel, Stefanie. "The Reading Brain: Differences between Digital and Print." *So Many Books*, 25 Apr. 2013, somanybooksblog.com/2013/04/25/the-reading-brain-differences-between-digital-and-print/.

A **song or other piece of music** on an album? Quotation marks.

Beyoncé. "Pretty Hurts." *Beyoncé*, Parkwood Entertainment, 2013, www.beyonce.com/album/beyonce/?media_view=songs.

Popular music follows the general rule: the title of a song is placed in quotation marks, and the title of an album is italicized. This remains true even when a track from an album is distributed by itself. If a piece of music released on its own is not originally part of a larger work, however, its title is italicized, regardless of how long the piece is.

When **a source is untitled**, provide a generic description of it, neither italicized nor enclosed in quotation marks, in place of a title. Capitalize the first word of the description and any proper nouns in it.

> Mackintosh, Charles Rennie. Chair of stained oak. 1897-1900, Victoria and Albert Museum, London.

The description may include the title of another work to which the one being documented is connected. Examples include the description of an untitled comment in an online forum (which incorporates the title of the article commented on) and the description of an untitled review (which incorporates the title of the work under review).

> Jeane. Comment on "The Reading Brain: Differences between Digital and Print." *So Many Books*, 25 Apr. 2013, 10:30 p.m., somanybooksblog.com/2013/04/25/the-reading-brain-differences-between-digital-and-print/#comment-83030.
>
> Mackin, Joseph. Review of *The Pleasures of Reading in an Age of Distraction*, by Alan Jacobs. *New York Journal of Books*, 2 June 2011, www.nyjournalofbooks.com/book-review/pleasures-reading-age-distraction.

Identify a short untitled message, such as a tweet, by reproducing its full text, without changes, in place of a title. Enclose the text in quotation marks.

> @persiankiwi. "We have report of large street battles in east & west of Tehran now - #Iranelection." *Twitter*, 23 June 2009, 11:15 a.m., twitter.com/persiankiwi/status/2298106072.

When you document an e-mail message, use its subject as the title. The subject is enclosed in quotation marks and its capitalization standardized.

*see sec. 1.2.1*

> Boyle, Anthony T. "Re: Utopia." Received by Daniel J. Cahill, 21 June 1997.

### 3 Title of container,

When the source being documented forms a part of a larger whole, the larger whole can be thought of as a container that holds the source. The container is crucial to the identification of the source. The title of the container is normally italicized and is followed by a comma, since the information that comes next describes the container.

The container may be a **book that is a collection** of essays, stories, poems, or other kinds of works.

Bazin, Patrick. "Toward Metareading." *The Future of the Book,* edited by Geoffrey Nunberg, U of California P, 1996, pp. 153-68.

Adding city to title of local newspaper
*see sec. 2.6.1*

It may be a **periodical** (journal, magazine, newspaper), which holds articles, creative writing, and so on.

Baron, Naomi S. "Redefining Reading: The Impact of Digital Communication Media." *PMLA,* vol. 128, no. 1, Jan. 2013, pp. 193-200.

Williams, Joy. "Rogue Territory." *The New York Times Book Review,* 9 Nov. 2014, pp. 1+.

Plus sign with page number
*see sec. 2.5.1*

Or a **television series**, which is made up of episodes.

"Hush." *Buffy the Vampire Slayer,* created by Joss Whedon, performance by Sarah Michelle Gellar, season 4, episode 10, Mutant Enemy, 1999.

Or a **Web site**, which contains articles, postings, and almost any other sort of work.

Hollmichel, Stefanie. "The Reading Brain: Differences between Digital and Print." *So Many Books,* 25 Apr. 2013, somanybooksblog.com/2013/04/25/the-reading-brain-differences-between-digital-and-print/.

An issue of a **comic book** is contained by the series of which it is part. If the issue also stands on its own, its title is italicized. In the Clowes example below, *David Boring* is the title of a stand-alone issue, while *Eightball* is the title of the series. In the Soule example, the issue and series are both titled *She-Hulk*; stating the issue title alone identifies the source sufficiently.

> Clowes, Daniel. *David Boring*. *Eightball*, no. 19, Fantagraphics, 1998.
>
> Soule, Charles, et al. *She-Hulk*. No. 1, Marvel Comics, 2014.

The above examples show works with one container. A container can, however, be nested in a larger container. A blog, for instance, may form part of a network of similar blogs. The complete back issues of a journal may be stored on a digital platform such as *JSTOR*. A book of short stories may be read on *Google Books*. A television series may be watched on a network like *Netflix*. Sometimes a source is part of two separate containers, both of which are relevant to your documentation. For example, an excerpt from a novel may be collected in a textbook of readings. Documenting the containers in which sources are found is increasingly important, as more and more works are retrieved through databases. Your reader needs to know where you found your sources since one copy of a work may differ from other copies.

It is usually best to account for all the containers that enclose your source, particularly when they are nested. Each container likely provides useful information for a reader seeking to understand and locate the original source. Add core elements 3–9 (from "Title of container" to "Location") to the end of the entry to account for each additional container. The examples on pages 32–36 use a template made up of the core elements to show you how to construct entries composed of two containers. (See the back of the book for a fill-in template that you can use to create entries.)

An article by Anne Goldman appeared in a journal, *The Georgia Review,* in 2010. Back issues of *The Georgia Review* are contained in *JSTOR*, an online database of journals and books.

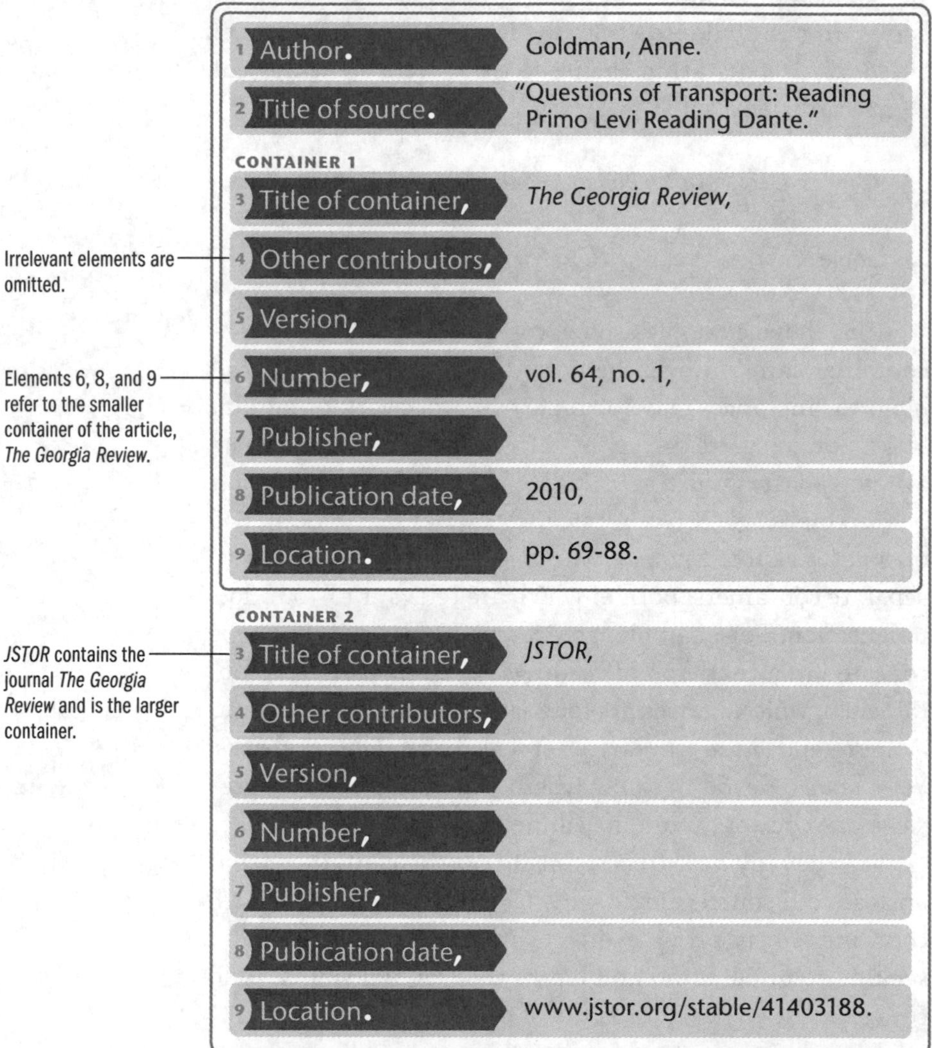

Irrelevant elements are omitted.
Elements 6, 8, and 9 refer to the smaller container of the article, *The Georgia Review*.
*JSTOR* contains the journal *The Georgia Review* and is the larger container.
1 Author. Goldman, Anne.
2 Title of source. "Questions of Transport: Reading Primo Levi Reading Dante."
CONTAINER 1
3 Title of container, *The Georgia Review,*
4 Other contributors,
5 Version,
6 Number, vol. 64, no. 1,
7 Publisher,
8 Publication date, 2010,
9 Location. pp. 69-88.
CONTAINER 2
3 Title of container, *JSTOR,*
4 Other contributors,
5 Version,
6 Number,
7 Publisher,
8 Publication date,
9 Location. www.jstor.org/stable/41403188.


Goldman, Anne. "Questions of Transport: Reading Primo Levi Reading Dante." *The Georgia Review,* vol. 64, no. 1, 2010, pp. 69-88. *JSTOR,* www.jstor.org/stable/41403188.

"Under the Gun," broadcast in 2013, is an episode in the television series *Pretty Little Liars*. The series was watched online through *Hulu*.

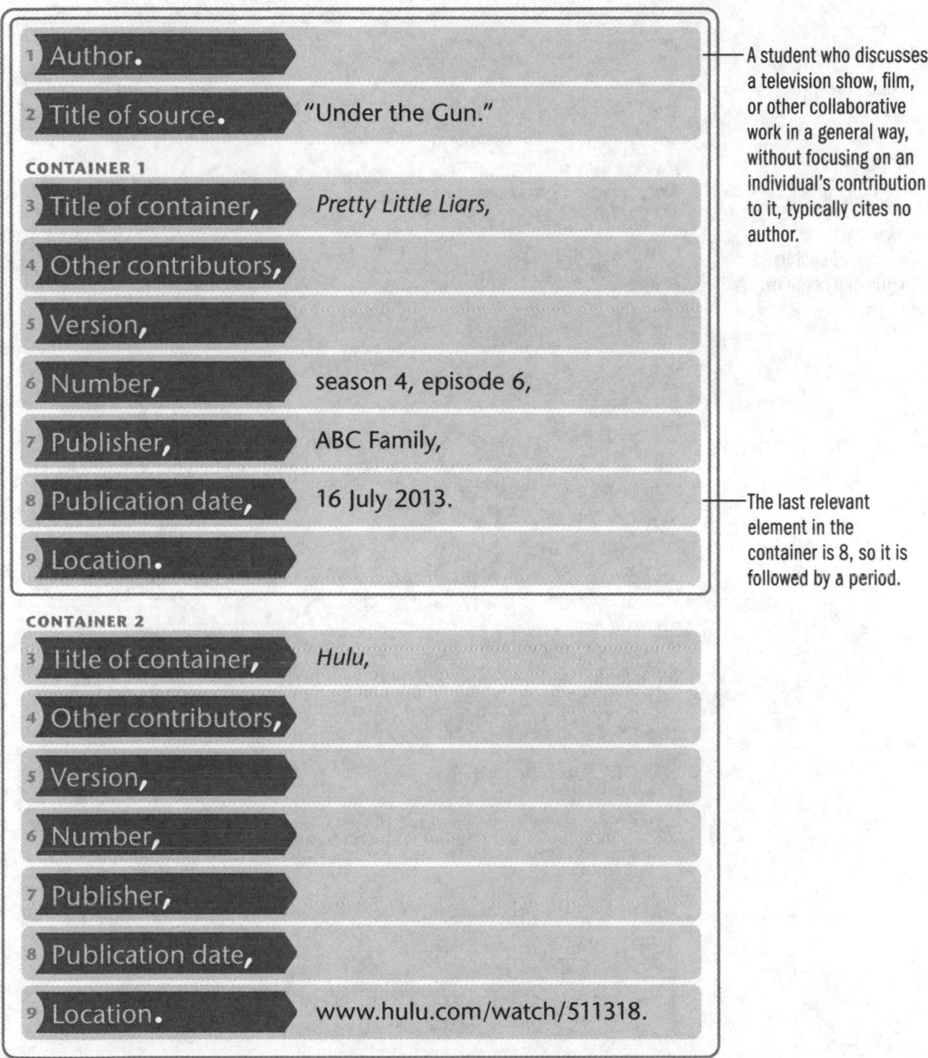

1 Author.
2 Title of source. "Under the Gun."
CONTAINER 1
3 Title of container, Pretty Little Liars,
4 Other contributors,
5 Version,
6 Number, season 4, episode 6,
7 Publisher, ABC Family,
8 Publication date, 16 July 2013.
9 Location.
CONTAINER 2
3 Title of container, Hulu,
4 Other contributors,
5 Version,
6 Number,
7 Publisher,
8 Publication date,
9 Location. www.hulu.com/watch/511318.
A student who discusses a television show, film, or other collaborative work in a general way, without focusing on an individual's contribution to it, typically cites no author.
The last relevant element in the container is 8, so it is followed by a period.


"Under the Gun." *Pretty Little Liars*, season 4, episode 6, ABC Family, 16 July 2013. *Hulu*, www.hulu.com/watch/511318.

Simon Gikandi's book *Ngugi wa Thiong'o*, a literary study, was published by Cambridge University Press in 2000 and is accessible online at *ACLS Humanities E-book*.

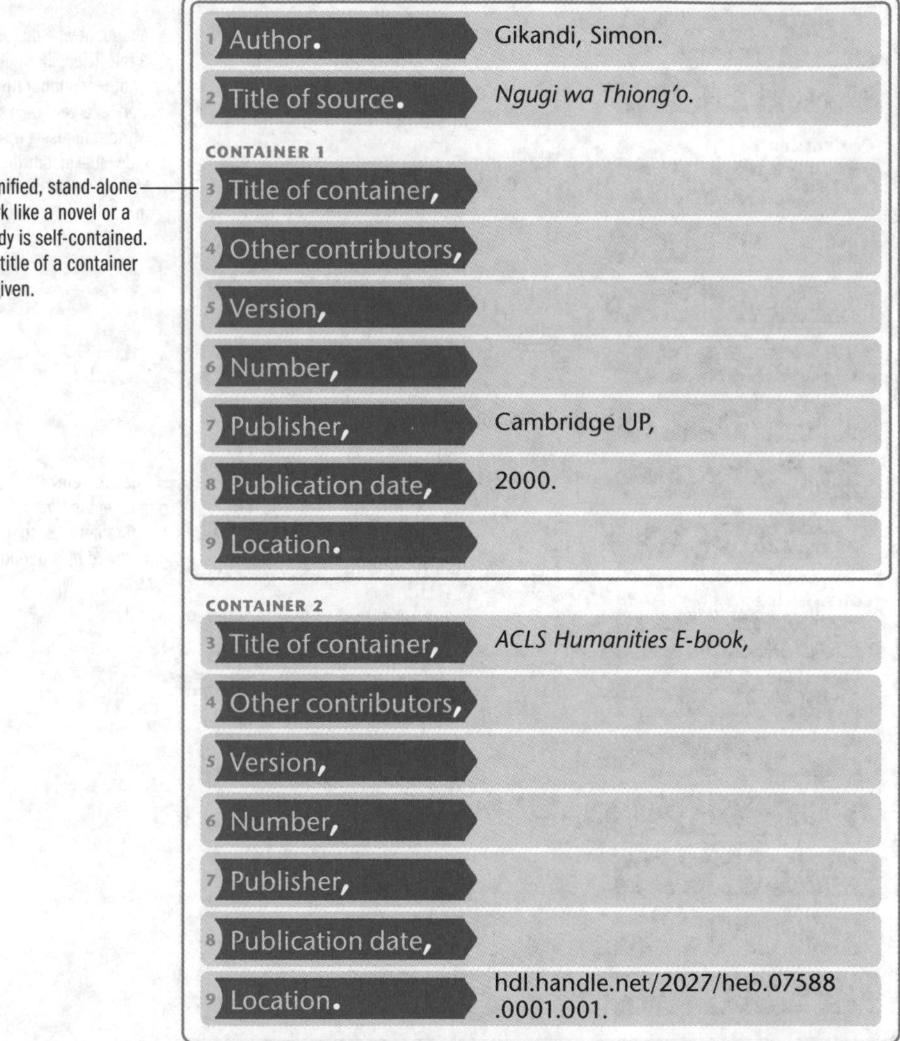

1 Author.
Gikandi, Simon.
2 Title of source.
Ngugi wa Thiong'o.
CONTAINER 1
A unified, stand-alone work like a novel or a study is self-contained. No title of a container is given.
3 Title of container,
4 Other contributors,
5 Version,
6 Number,
7 Publisher,
Cambridge UP,
8 Publication date,
2000.
9 Location.
CONTAINER 2
3 Title of container,
ACLS Humanities E-book,
4 Other contributors,
5 Version,
6 Number,
7 Publisher,
8 Publication date,
9 Location.
hdl.handle.net/2027/heb.07588
.0001.001.


Gikandi, Simon. *Ngugi wa Thiong'o.* Cambridge UP, 2000. *ACLS Humanities E-book*, hdl.handle.net/2027/heb.07588.0001.001.

A short story by Edgar Allan Poe is included in volume 4 of a multi-volume edition of his complete works that was published in 1902. The edition is available at *HathiTrust Digital Library*.

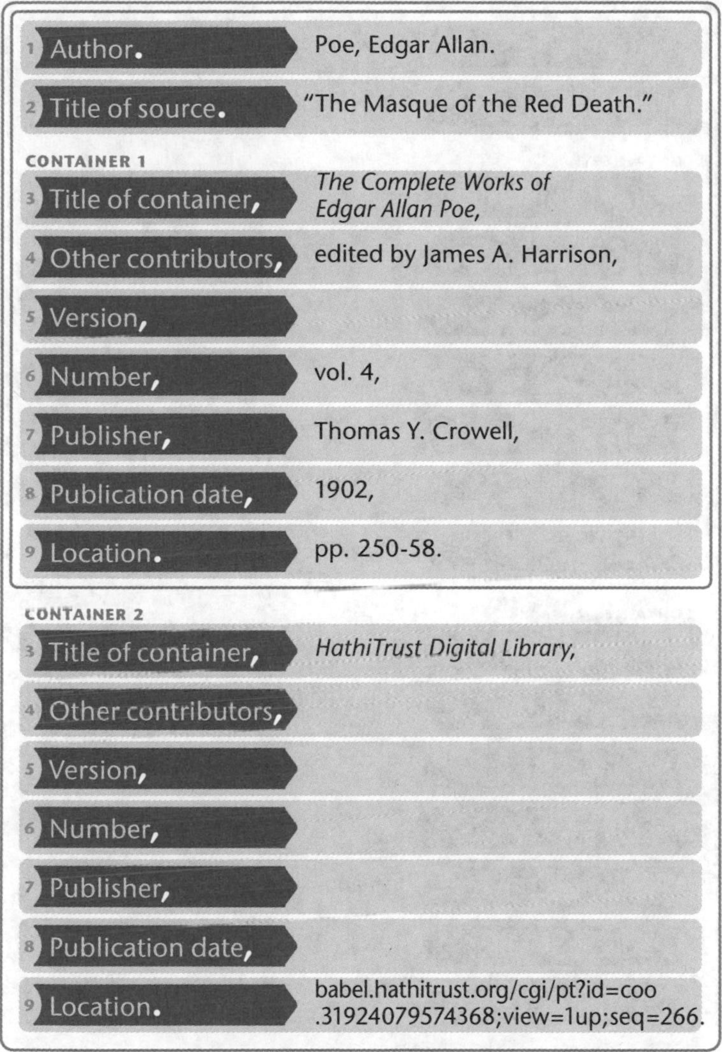

1 Author.
Poe, Edgar Allan.
2 Title of source.
"The Masque of the Red Death."
CONTAINER 1
3 Title of container,
The Complete Works of Edgar Allan Poe,
4 Other contributors,
edited by James A. Harrison,
5 Version,
6 Number,
vol. 4,
7 Publisher,
Thomas Y. Crowell,
8 Publication date,
1902,
9 Location.
pp. 250-58.
CONTAINER 2
3 Title of container,
HathiTrust Digital Library,
4 Other contributors,
5 Version,
6 Number,
7 Publisher,
8 Publication date,
9 Location.
babel.hathitrust.org/cgi/pt?id=coo.31924079574368;view=1up;seq=266.


Poe, Edgar Allan. "The Masque of the Red Death." *The Complete Works of Edgar Allan Poe,* edited by James A. Harrison, vol. 4, Thomas Y. Crowell, 1902, pp. 250-58. *HathiTrust Digital Library,* babel.hathitrust.org/cgi/pt?id=coo.31924079574368;view=1up;seq=266.

A novel by W. D. Howells takes up all of volume 5 of a multivolume edition of his works published by Indiana University Press. The volumes in the edition were published over a span of years.

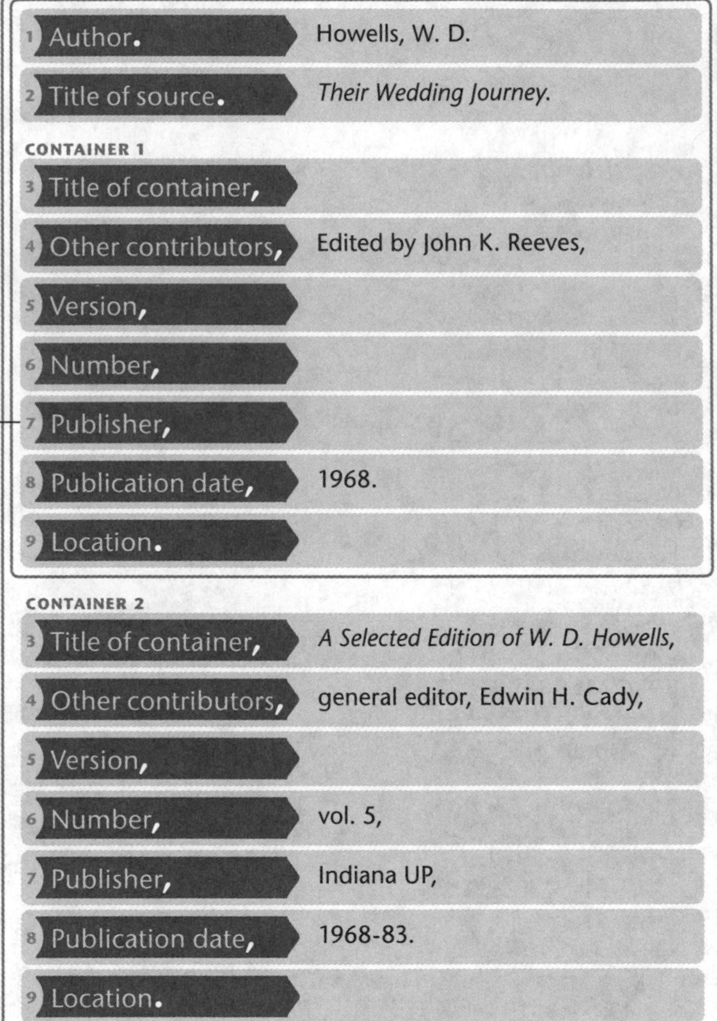


When a publication fact applies to more than one container, the fact is cited in the last relevant container. Hence, the publisher is omitted here and included in container 2.

There may be more than one correct entry for a source. The facts here about the multivolume edition (container 2) would be useful in some projects, but in a project where the documentation serves only to identify the sources used, this minimal entry would be acceptable:

Howells, W. D. *Their Wedding Journey*. Edited by John K. Reeves, Indiana UP, 1968.

Howells, W. D. *Their Wedding Journey.* Edited by John K. Reeves, 1968. *A Selected Edition of W. D. Howells*, general editor, Edwin H. Cady, vol. 5, Indiana UP, 1968-83.

## 4 Other contributors,

Aside from an author whose name appears at the start of the entry, other people may be credited in the source as contributors. If their participation is important to your research or to the identification of the work, name the other contributors in the entry. Precede each name (or each group of names, if more than one person performed the same function) with a description of the role. Below are common descriptions.

adapted by
directed by
edited by
illustrated by
introduction by
narrated by
performance by
translated by

A few other kinds of contributors (e.g., guest editors, general editors) cannot be described with a phrase like those above. The role must instead be expressed as a noun followed by a comma.

general editor, Edwin H. Cady

The **editors** of scholarly editions and of collections and the **translators** of works originally published in another language are usually recorded in documentation because they play key roles.

Chartier, Roger. *The Order of Books: Readers, Authors, and Libraries in Europe between the Fourteenth and Eighteenth Centuries.* Translated by Lydia G. Cochrane, Stanford UP, 1994.

Dewar, James A., and Peng Hwa Ang. "The Cultural Consequences of Printing and the Internet." *Agent*

When three or more other contributors perform the same function, give the name that is listed first in the source and follow it with *et al.*

*of Change: Print Culture Studies after Elizabeth L. Eisenstein*, edited by Sabrina Alcorn Baron et al., U of Massachusetts P / Center for the Book, Library of Congress, 2007, pp. 365-77.

If a source such as a film, television episode, or performance has **many contributors**, include the ones most relevant to your project. For example, if you are writing about a television episode and focus on a key character, you might mention the series creator and the actor who portrays the character.

"Hush." *Buffy the Vampire Slayer*, created by Joss Whedon, performance by Sarah Michelle Gellar, season 4, episode 10, Mutant Enemy, 1999.

A source contained in a collection may have a **contributor who did not play a role in the entire collection**. For instance, stories and poems in an anthology are often translated by various hands. Identify such a contributor after the title of the source rather than after that of the collection.

Fagih, Ahmed Ibrahim al-. *The Singing of the Stars*. Translated by Leila El Khalidi and Christopher Tingley. *Short Arabic Plays: An Anthology*, edited by Salma Khadra Jayyusi, Interlink Books, 2003, pp. 140-57.

## 5 Version,

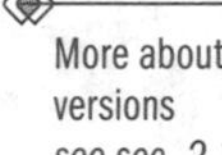

More about versions *see sec. 2.3*

If the source carries a notation indicating that it is a version of a work released in more than one form, identify the version in your entry. Books are commonly issued in versions called *editions*. A revised version of a book may be labeled *revised edition* or be numbered (*second edition*, etc.). Versions of books are sometimes given other descriptions as well.

*The Bible*. Authorized King James Version, Oxford UP, 1998.

Cheyfitz, Eric. *The Poetics of Imperialism: Translation and Colonization from* The Tempest *to* Tarzan. Expanded ed., U of Pennsylvania P, 1997.

Miller, Casey, and Kate Swift. *Words and Women.* Updated ed., HarperCollins Publishers, 1991.

Newcomb, Horace, editor. *Television: The Critical View.* 7th ed., Oxford UP, 2007.

Works in other media may also appear in versions.

Schubert, Franz. *Piano Trio in E Flat Major D 929.* Performance by Wiener Mozart-Trio, unabridged version, Deutsch 929, Preiser Records, 2011.

Scott, Ridley, director. *Blade Runner.* 1982. Performance by Harrison Ford, director's cut, Warner Bros., 1992.

Shakespeare, William. *The Tragedy of Othello.* Edited by Barbara Mowat and Paul Werstine, version 1.3.1, Luminary Digital Media, 2013.

## 6 Number,

More about numbers see sec. 1.4

The source you are documenting may be part of a numbered sequence. A text too long to be printed in one book, for instance, is issued in multiple volumes, which may be numbered. If you consult **one volume of a numbered multivolume set**, indicate the volume number.

Rampersad, Arnold. *The Life of Langston Hughes.* 2nd ed., vol. 2, Oxford UP, 2002.

Wellek, René. *A History of Modern Criticism, 1750-1950.* Vol. 5, Yale UP, 1986.

**Journal issues** are typically numbered. Some journals use both **volume and issue numbers**. In general, the issues of a journal published in a single year compose one volume. Usually, volumes are numbered sequentially, while the numbering of issues starts over with 1 in each new volume.

Baron, Naomi S. "Redefining Reading: The Impact of Digital Communication Media." *PMLA*, vol. 128, no. 1, Jan. 2013, pp. 193-200.

Other journals do not use volume numbers but instead number all the issues in sequence.

Kafka, Ben. "The Demon of Writing: Paperwork, Public Safety, and the Reign of Terror." *Representations*, no. 98, 2007, pp. 1-24.

**Comic books** are commonly numbered like journals—for instance, with issue numbers.

Clowes, Daniel. *David Boring. Eightball*, no. 19, Fantagraphics, 1998.

The **seasons of a television series** are typically numbered in sequence, as are the **episodes** in a season. Both numbers should be recorded in the works-cited list if available.

"Hush." *Buffy the Vampire Slayer*, created by Joss Whedon, performance by Sarah Michelle Gellar, season 4, episode 10, Mutant Enemy, 1999.

If your source uses another numbering system, include the number in your entry, preceded by a term that identifies the kind of division the number refers to.

More about publishers *see secs. 1.6.3, 2.4*

## 7 Publisher,

The publisher is the organization primarily responsible for producing the source or making it available to the public. If two or more organizations are named in the source and they seem equally responsible for the work, cite each of them, separating the names with a forward slash (/). But if one of the organizations had primary responsibility for the work, cite it alone.

To determine the publisher of a **book**, look first on the title page. If no publisher's name appears there, look on the copyright page (usually the reverse of the title page).

> Jacobs, Alan. *The Pleasures of Reading in an Age of Distraction.* Oxford UP, 2011.
>
> Lessig, Lawrence. *Remix: Making Art and Commerce Thrive in the Hybrid Economy.* Penguin Press, 2008.

**Films and television series** are often produced and distributed by several companies performing different tasks. When documenting a work in film or television, you should generally cite the organization that had the primary overall responsibility for it.

> Kuzui, Fran Rubel, director. *Buffy the Vampire Slayer.* Twentieth Century Fox, 1992.

**Web sites** are published by various kinds of organizations, including museums, libraries, and universities and their departments. The publisher's name can often be found in a copyright notice at the bottom of the home page or on a page that gives information about the site.

> Harris, Charles "Teenie." *Woman in Paisley Shirt behind Counter in Record Store. Teenie Harris Archive,* Carnegie Museum of Art, Pittsburgh, teenie.cmoa.org/interactive/index.html#date08.
>
> *Manifold Greatness: The Creation and Afterlife of the King James Bible.* Folger Shakespeare Library / Bodleian Libraries, U of Oxford / Harry Ransom Center, U of Texas, Austin, manifoldgreatness.org.

A **blog network** may be considered the publisher of the blogs it hosts.

Clancy, Kate. "Defensive Scholarly Writing and Science Communication." *Context and Variation*, Scientific American Blogs, 24 Apr. 2013, blogs.scientificamerican .com/context-and-variation/2013/04/24/defensive-scholarly-writing-and-science-communication/.

A publisher's name may be omitted for the following kinds of publications, either because the publisher need not be given or because there is no publisher.

- A periodical (journal, magazine, newspaper)
- A work published by its author or editor
- A Web site whose title is essentially the same as the name of its publisher
- A Web site not involved in producing the works it makes available (e.g., a service for users' content like *WordPress.com* or *YouTube*, an archive like *JSTOR* or *ProQuest*). If the contents of the site are organized into a whole, as the contents of *YouTube*, *JSTOR*, and *ProQuest* are, the site is named earlier as a container, but it still does not qualify as a publisher of the source.

## 8 Publication date,

Sources—especially those published online—may be associated with more than one publication date. For instance, an article collected in a book may be accompanied by a note saying that the article appeared years earlier in a journal. A work online may have been published previously in another medium (as a book, a broadcast television program, a record album, etc.).

When a source carries more than one date, cite the date that is most meaningful or most relevant to your use of the source. For example, if you consult an **article on the Web site of a news organization** that also publishes its articles in print, the date of online publication may appear at the site along with the date when the article appeared in print. Since you consulted only the online version of the article, ignore the date of the print publication.

> Deresiewicz, William. "The Death of the Artist—and the Birth of the Creative Entrepreneur." *The Atlantic*, 28 Dec. 2014, www.theatlantic.com/magazine/archive/2015/01/the-death-of-the-artist-and-the-birth-of-the-creative-entrepreneur/383497/.

A reader of the print version would find only one date of publication in the source and would produce the following entry.

> Deresiewicz, William. "The Death of the Artist—and the Birth of the Creative Entrepreneur." *The Atlantic*, Jan.-Feb. 2015, pp. 92-97.

Whether to give the year alone or to include a month and day usually depends on your source: write the full date as you find it there. Occasionally, you must decide how full the cited date will be. For instance, if you are documenting an **episode of a television series**, the year of its original release may suffice.

> "Hush." *Buffy the Vampire Slayer*, created by Joss Whedon, performance by Sarah Michelle Gellar, season 4, episode 10, Mutant Enemy, 1999.

"Mutant Enemy," in the first example for "Hush," is the primary production company. In the second example, we replaced it with "WB Television Network" (on which the episode originally aired), in keeping with the decision to specify the date of airing.

However, if you are discussing, say, the historical context in which the episode originally aired, you may want to supply the month and day along with the year.

> "Hush." *Buffy the Vampire Slayer*, created by Joss Whedon, performance by Sarah Michelle Gellar, season 4, episode 10, WB Television Network, 14 Dec. 1999.

If you are exploring features of that episode found on the season's **DVD set**, your entry will be about the discs and thus will include the date of their release.

In this version, the container title is that of the DVD set.

"Hush." 1999. *Buffy the Vampire Slayer: The Complete Fourth Season*, created by Joss Whedon, performance by Sarah Michelle Gellar, episode 10, Twentieth Century Fox, 2003, disc 3.

An entry for a **video on a Web site** includes the date when the video was posted there.

This example omits the creator, the performer, and other facts about the series because they are not stated in this source.

"*Buffy the Vampire Slayer*: Unaired Pilot 1996." *YouTube*, uploaded by Brian Stowe, 28 Jan. 2012, www.youtube.com/watch?v=WR3J-v7QXXw.

Many kinds of **articles on the Web** plainly carry dates of publication.

Hollmichel, Stefanie. "The Reading Brain: Differences between Digital and Print." *So Many Books*, 25 Apr. 2013, somanybooksblog.com/2013/04/25/the-reading-brain-differences-between-digital-and-print/.

**Comments posted on Web pages** are usually dated. If an article, a comment, or another source on the Web includes a time when the work was posted or last modified, include the time along with the date.

Jeane. Comment on "The Reading Brain: Differences between Digital and Print." *So Many Books*, 25 Apr. 2013, 10:30 p.m., somanybooksblog.com/2013/04/25/the-reading-brain-differences-between-digital-and-print/#comment-83030.

When you document a **Web project as a whole**, cite a range of dates if the project was developed over time.

Eaves, Morris, et al., editors. *The William Blake Archive*. 1996-2014, www.blakearchive.org/blake/.

An **issue of a periodical** (journal, magazine, newspaper) usually carries a date on its cover or title page. Periodicals vary in their publication schedules: issues may appear every year, season, month, week, or day.

Baron, Naomi S. "Redefining Reading: The Impact of Digital Communication Media." *PMLA*, vol. 128, no. 1, Jan. 2013, pp. 193-200.

Belton, John. "Painting by the Numbers: The Digital Intermediate." *Film Quarterly*, vol. 61, no. 3, Spring 2008, pp. 58-65.

Kafka, Ben. "The Demon of Writing: Paperwork, Public Safety, and the Reign of Terror." *Representations*, no. 98, 2007, pp. 1-24.

Seasons in the works-cited list *see sec. 1.5*

When documenting a **book**, look for the date of publication on the title page. If the title page lacks a date, check the book's copyright page (usually the reverse of the title page). If more than one date appears on the copyright page, select the most recent one (see fig. 5).

Optionally citing a date of original publication *see pp. 50-51*

Ellison, Ralph. *Invisible Man*. Vintage Books, 1995.

The second and later editions of a book may contain the dates of all the editions. Cite the date of the edition you used, normally the date on the title page or the last date listed on the copyright page. Do not take the publication dates of books from an outside resource—such as a bibliography, an online catalog, or a bookseller like *Amazon*—since the information there may be inaccurate (see fig. 6).

SECOND VINTAGE INTERNATIONAL EDITION, MARCH 1995

*Copyright 1947, 1948, 1952 by Ralph Ellison*

*Copyright renewed 1980 by Ralph Ellison*

All rights reserved under International and Pan-American Copyright Conventions. Published in the United States by Random House, Inc., New York, and simultaneously in Canada by Random House of Canada Limited, Toronto. Originally published by Random House, Inc., in 1952.

Library of Congress Cataloging in Publication Data
Ellison, Ralph.
Invisible man.
I. Title.
[PZ4.E47In5] [PS3555.Lb25] 813'.54 72-10419
ISBN 0-679-73276-4

*Book design by Cathryn S. Aison*

Manufactured in the United States of America
3579C8642

**Fig. 5.** The copyright page of a book. There is no publication date on the title page of this book.

More about locations
*see sec. 2.5*

## 9 Location.

How to specify a work's location depends on the medium of publication. In print sources **a page number** (preceded by *p.*) **or a range of page numbers** (preceded by *pp.*) specifies the location of a text in a container such as a book anthology or a periodical.

Adichie, Chimamanda Ngozi. "On Monday of Last Week." *The Thing around Your Neck*, Alfred A. Knopf, 2009, pp. 74-94.

Baron, Naomi S. "Redefining Reading: The Impact of Digital Communication Media." *PMLA*, vol. 128, no. 1, Jan. 2013, pp. 193-200.

Deresiewicz, William. "The Death of the Artist—and the Birth of the Creative Entrepreneur." *The Atlantic*, Jan.-Feb. 2015, pp. 92-97.

El ingenioso hidalgo Don Quijote de la Mancha, compuesto por Miguel de Cervantes Saavedra y comentado por D. Diego Clemencín. v.3

by Cervantes Saavedra, Miguel de, 1547-1616.
Published 1984

Catalog Record   Full view

Publication date according to online database

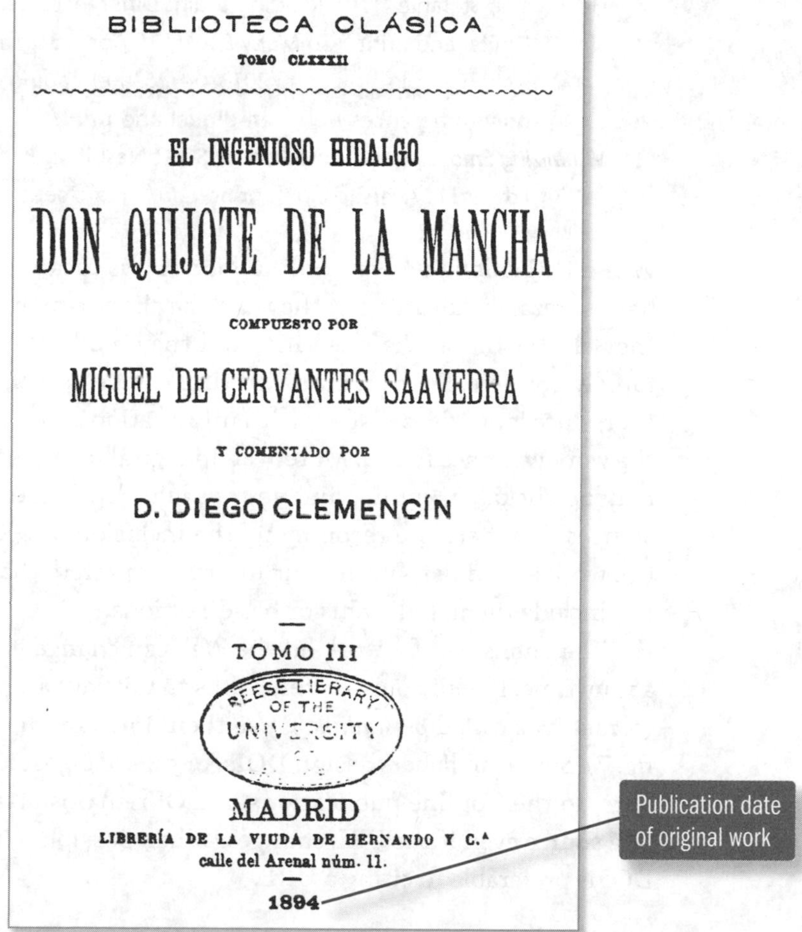

BIBLIOTECA CLÁSICA

TOMO CLXXXII

EL INGENIOSO HIDALGO

DON QUIJOTE DE LA MANCHA

COMPUESTO POR

MIGUEL DE CERVANTES SAAVEDRA

Y COMENTADO POR

D. DIEGO CLEMENCÍN

TOMO III



MADRID

LIBRERÍA DE LA VIUDA DE HERNANDO Y C.ª

calle del Arenal núm. 11.

1894



**Fig. 6.** The listing for a book in an online database (*above*) and the title page of the book (*below*). The book was published in 1894, but the database incorrectly shows 1984 as the publication date. Publication facts should be taken from the work itself, not from another source.

The location of an online work is commonly indicated by its **URL**, or Web address.

> Deresiewicz, William. "The Death of the Artist—and the Birth of the Creative Entrepreneur." *The Atlantic*, 28 Dec. 2014, www.theatlantic.com/magazine/archive/2015/01/the-death-of-the-artist-and-the-birth-of-the-creative-entrepreneur/383497/.
>
> Hollmichel, Stefanie. "The Reading Brain: Differences between Digital and Print." *So Many Books*, 25 Apr. 2013, somanybooksblog.com/2013/04/25/the-reading-brain-differences-between-digital-and-print/.
>
> *Visualizing Emancipation*. Directed by Scott Nesbit and Edward L. Ayers, dsl.richmond.edu/emancipation/.

While URLs define where online material is located, they have several disadvantages: they can't be clicked on in print, they clutter the works-cited list, and they tend to become rapidly obsolete. Even an outdated URL can be useful, however, since it provides readers with information about where the work was once found. Moreover, in digital formats URLs may be clickable, connecting your reader directly to your sources. We therefore recommend the inclusion of URLs in the works-cited list, but if your instructor prefers that you not include them, follow his or her directions.

The publisher of a work on the Web can change its URL at any time. If your source offers URLs that it says are stable (sometimes called *permalinks*), use them in your entry (see fig. 7). Some publishers assign **DOIs**, or digital object identifiers, to their online publications. A DOI remains attached to a source even if the URL changes. When possible, citing a DOI is preferable to citing a URL.

> Chan, Evans. "Postmodernism and Hong Kong Cinema." *Postmodern Culture*, vol. 10, no. 3, May 2000. *Project Muse*, doi:10.1353/pmc.2000.0021.

URLs and DOIs
*see sec. 2.5.2*

The location of a television episode in a DVD set is indicated by the **disc number**.

> "Hush." *Buffy the Vampire Slayer: The Complete Fourth Season*, created by Joss Whedon, performance by Sarah Michelle Gellar, episode 10, WB Television Network, 2003, disc 3.

A physical object that you experienced firsthand (not in a reproduction), such as a work of art in a museum or an artifact in an archive, is located in a **place**, commonly an institution. Give the name of the place and of its city (but omit the city if it is part of the place's name).

> Bearden, Romare. *The Train.* 1975, Museum of Modern Art, New York.

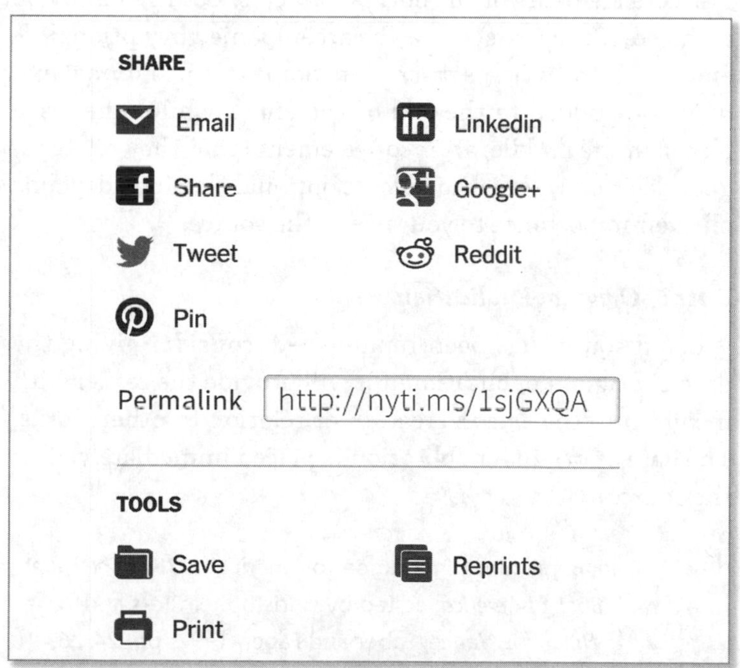


**Fig. 7.** The stable URL of a Web page. The features for using the page include a "permalink," a URL that the publisher promises not to change.

The location of an object in an archive may also include a **number or other code** that the archive uses to identify the object.

> Chaucer, Geoffrey. *The Canterbury Tales*. Circa 1400-10, British Library, London, Harley MS 7334.

Record the location of a performance, a lecture, or another form of live presentation by naming the **venue and its city** (but omit the city if it is part of the venue's name).

> Atwood, Margaret. "Silencing the Scream." Boundaries of the Imagination Forum. MLA Annual Convention, 29 Dec. 1993, Royal York Hotel, Toronto.

## Optional Elements

The core elements of the entry—which should generally be included, if they exist—may be accompanied by optional elements, at the writer's discretion. Some of the optional elements are added to the end of the entry, while others are placed in the middle, after core elements that they relate to. Your decision whether to include optional elements depends on their importance to your use of the source.

### *Date of Original Publication*

When a source has been republished, consider giving the date of original publication if it will provide the reader with insight into the work's creation or relation to other works. The date of original publication is placed immediately after the source's title.

> Franklin, Benjamin. "Emigration to America." 1782. *The Faber Book of America*, edited by Christopher Ricks and William L. Vance, Faber and Faber, 1992, pp. 24-26.
>
> Newcomb, Horace, editor. *Television: The Critical View*. 1976. 7th ed., Oxford UP, 2007.

Scott, Ridley, director. *Blade Runner.* 1982. Performance by Harrison Ford, director's cut, Warner Bros., 1992.

### *City of Publication*

The traditional practice of citing the city where the publisher of a book was located usually serves little purpose today. There remain a few circumstances in which the city of publication might matter, however.

Books published before 1900 are conventionally associated with their cities of publication. In an entry for a pre-1900 work, you may give the city of publication in place of the publisher's name.

Goethe, Johann Wolfgang von. *Conversations of Goethe with Eckermann and Soret*. Translated by John Oxenford, new ed., London, 1875.

In addition, a publisher with offices in more than one country may release a novel in two versions—perhaps with different spelling and vocabulary. If you read an unexpected version of a text (such as the British edition when you are in the United States), stating the city of publication will help your readers understand your source. Place the name of the city before that of the publisher.

Rowling, J. K. *Harry Potter and the Philosopher's Stone.* London, Bloomsbury, 1997.

Finally, include the city of publication whenever it might help a reader locate a text released by an unfamiliar publisher located outside North America.

### *Other Facts about the Source*

There may be other information that will help your reader track down the original source. You might, for instance, include the total number of volumes in a **multivolume publication**.

Caro, Robert A. *The Passage of Power.* 2012. *The Years of Lyndon Johnson,* vol. 4, Vintage Books, 1982- . 4 vols.

Rampersad, Arnold. *The Life of Langston Hughes.* 2nd ed., Oxford UP, 2002. 2 vols.

Wellek, René. *A History of Modern Criticism, 1750-1950.* Vol. 8, Yale UP, 1992. 8 vols.

If the title page or a preceding page indicates that a book you are documenting is part of a **series**, you might include the series name, neither italicized nor enclosed in quotation marks, and the number of the book (if any) in the series.

Kuhnheim, Jill S. "Cultures of the Lyric and Lyrical Culture: Teaching Poetry and Cultural Studies." *Cultural Studies in the Curriculum: Teaching Latin America,* edited by Danny J. Anderson and Kuhnheim, MLA, 2003, pp. 105-22. Teaching Languages, Literatures, and Cultures.

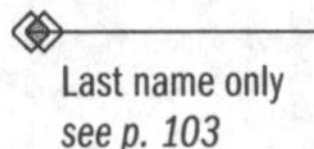

Last name only
*see p. 103*

Neruda, Pablo. *Canto General.* Translated by Jack Schmitt, U of California P, 1991. Latin American Literature and Culture 7.

If the source is an **unexpected type of work**, you may identify the type with a descriptive term. For instance, if you studied a speech by reading its transcript, the term *Transcript* will indicate that you did not listen to the speech.

Allende, Isabel. "Tales of Passion." *TED: Ideas Worth Spreading,* Jan. 2008, www.ted.com/talks/isabel_allende_tells_tales_of_passion/transcript?language=en. Transcript.

Similarly, a **lecture or other address** heard in person may be indicated as such.

Atwood, Margaret. "Silencing the Scream." Boundaries of the Imagination Forum. MLA Annual Convention, 29 Dec. 1993, Royal York Hotel, Toronto. Address.

When a source was previously published in a form other than the one in which you consulted it, you might include **information about the prior publication**.

> Johnson, Barbara. "My Monster / My Self." *The Barbara Johnson Reader: The Surprise of Otherness*, edited by Melissa Feuerstein et al., Duke UP, 2014, pp. 179-90. Originally published in *Diacritics*, vol. 12, no. 2, 1982, pp. 2-10.

When documenting a bill, report, or resolution of the **United States Congress**, you might include the number and session of Congress from which it emerged and specify the document's type and number.

see sec. 2.1.3

> United States, Congress, House, Permanent Select Committee on Intelligence. *Al-Qaeda: The Many Faces of an Islamist Extremist Threat.* Government Printing Office, 2006. 109th Congress, 2nd session, House Report 615.

### *Date of Access*

Since online works typically can be changed or removed at any time, the date on which you accessed online material is often an important indicator of the version you consulted.

> "Under the Gun." *Pretty Little Liars*, season 4, episode 6, ABC Family, 16 July 2013. *Hulu*, www.hulu.com/watch/511318. Accessed 23 July 2013.

The date of access is especially crucial if the source provides no date specifying when it was produced or published.

This list of optional elements is not exhaustive. You should carefully consider the source you are documenting and judge whether other kinds of information might help your reader.

## In-Text Citations

The second major component of MLA documentation style is the insertion in your text of a brief reference that indicates the source you consulted. The in-text citation should direct the reader unambiguously to the entry in your works-cited list for the source—and, if possible, to a passage in the source—while creating the least possible interruption in your text.

A typical in-text citation is composed of the element that comes first in the entry in the works-cited list (usually the author's name) and a page number. The page number goes in a parenthesis, which is placed, when possible, where there is a natural pause in the text. A parenthetical citation that directly follows a quotation is placed after the closing quotation mark. The other item (usually the author's name) may appear in the text itself or, abbreviated, before the page number in the parenthesis.

> According to Naomi Baron, reading is "just half of literacy. The other half is writing" (194). One might even suggest that reading is never complete without writing.

or

> Reading is "just half of literacy. The other half is writing" (Baron 194). One might even suggest that reading is never complete without writing.

Work Cited

Baron, Naomi S. "Redefining Reading: The Impact of Digital Communication Media." *PMLA*, vol. 128, no. 1, Jan. 2013, pp. 193-200.

A reader interested in your source can flip to the indicated entry in your list of works cited; a reader not interested in the source can pass over the citation without being distracted. Rarely should the page number be mentioned in the text (e.g., "As Naomi Baron argues on page 194") since it would disrupt the flow of ideas.

When a quotation, whether of prose or poetry, is so long that it is set off from the text, type a space after the concluding punctuation mark of the quotation and insert the parenthetical citation.

Long prose and poetry quotations see secs. 1.3.2–3

> The forms of writing that accompany reading
>
> > can fill various roles. The simplest is to make parts of a text prominent (by underlining, highlighting, or adding asterisks, lines, or squiggles). More-reflective responses are notes written in the margins or in an external location—a notebook or a computer file. (Baron 194)
>
> All these forms of writing bear in common the reader's desire to add to, complete, or even alter the text.

There are circumstances in which a citation like "(Baron 194)" doesn't provide enough information to lead unambiguously to a specific entry. If you borrow from works by more than one author with the same last name (e.g., Naomi Baron and Sabrina Alcorn Baron), eliminate ambiguity in the citation by adding the author's first initial (or, if the initial is shared too, the full first name).

> Reading is "just half of literacy. The other half is writing" (N. Baron 194). One might even suggest that reading is never complete without writing.

Even if you cite only one author named Baron in your text, "(Baron 194)" is insufficient if more than one work appears under that author's name in the works-cited list. In that case, include a short form of the source's title.

see sec. 3.2.1

> Reading is "just half of literacy. The other half is writing" (Baron, "Redefining" 194). One might even suggest that reading is never complete without writing.

When an entry in the works-cited list begins with the title of the work—either because the work is anonymous or because

see p. 24

see sec. 2.1.3

its author is the organization that published it—your in-text citation contains the title. The title may appear in the text itself or, abbreviated, before the page number in the parenthesis.

> *Reading at Risk: A Survey of Literary Reading in America* notes that despite an apparent decline in reading during the same period, "the number of people doing creative writing—of any genre, not exclusively literary works—increased substantially between 1982 and 2002" (3).

or

> Despite an apparent decline in reading during the same period, "the number of people doing creative writing—of any genre, not exclusively literary works—increased substantially between 1982 and 2002" (*Reading* 3).

Work Cited

*Reading at Risk: A Survey of Literary Reading in America.* National Endowment for the Arts, June 2004. Research Division Report 46.

If your source uses explicit paragraph numbers rather than page numbers—as some publications on the Web do—give the relevant number or numbers, preceded by the label *par.* or *pars.* Change the label appropriately if another kind of part is numbered in the source instead of pages, such as sections (*sec.*, *secs.*) or chapters (*ch.*, *chs.*). If the author's name begins such a citation, place a comma after the name.

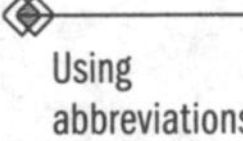

Using abbreviations
see sec. 1.6

> There is little evidence here for the claim that "Eagleton has belittled the gains of postmodernism" (Chan, par. 41).

When a source has no page numbers or any other kind of part number, no number should be given in a parenthetical citation. Do not count unnumbered paragraphs or other parts.

> "As we read we . . . construct the terrain of a book" (Hollmichel), something that is more difficult when the text reflows on a screen.

In parenthetical citations of a literary work available in multiple editions, such as a commonly studied novel, play, or poem, it is often helpful to provide division numbers in addition to, or instead of, page numbers, so that readers can find your references in any edition of the work.

see sec. 3.3.2

> Austen begins the final chapter of *Mansfield Park* with a dismissive "Let other pens dwell," thereby announcing her decision to avoid dwelling on the professions of love made by Fanny and Edmund (533; vol. 3, ch. 17).

For works in time-based media, such as audio and video recordings, cite the relevant time or range of times. Give the numbers of the hours, minutes, and seconds as displayed in your media player, separating the numbers with colons.

> Buffy's promise that "there's not going to be any incidents like at my old school" is obviously not one on which she can follow through ("*Buffy*" 00:03:16-17).

Identifying the source in your text is essential for nearly every kind of borrowing—not only quotations but also facts and paraphrased ideas. (The only exception is common knowledge.) The parenthetical citation for a fact or paraphrased idea should be placed as close as possible after the borrowed material, at a natural pause in your sentence, so that the flow of your argument is not disrupted.

see p. 10

> While reading may be the core of literacy, Naomi Baron argues that literacy can be complete only when reading is accompanied by writing (194).

or

> While reading may be the core of literacy, literacy can be complete only when reading is accompanied by writing (Baron 194).

The second version above is usually preferable when a single fact or paraphrased idea is attributable to more than one source. List all the sources in the parenthetical citation, separating them with semicolons.

> While reading may be the core of literacy, literacy can be complete only when reading is accompanied by writing (Baron 194; Jacobs 55).

Remember that the goal of the in-text citation is to provide enough information to lead your reader directly to the source you used while disrupting the flow of your argument as little as possible.

# PART 2

# Details of MLA Style

# Introduction

Part 1 of this handbook describes the general principles for documenting research sources in any medium or format. While this mode of citation provides a great deal of flexibility, it nonetheless requires that writers be consistent to avoid confusing the reader. In part 2, accordingly, we address the role of consistency by shifting our emphasis from the descriptive to the prescriptive, first offering recommendations about the mechanics of prose in a research project and then discussing advanced aspects of the works-cited list and in-text citations in MLA style. Finally, part 2 considers citations in projects other than the research paper.

# 1 The Mechanics of Scholarly Prose

Conventions in academic writing enable readers to focus their attention on what is most important: the author's argument. Following are some of the conventions commonly accepted in scholarly writing.

## 1.1 Names of Persons

### 1.1.1 First and Subsequent Uses of Names

With the exception of very famous persons (such as Shakespeare or Dante), state someone's name fully the first time you use it in your discussion. Write the name accurately, exactly as it appears in your source or in a reference work.

Gabriel García Márquez
Li Ang
Arthur George Rust, Jr.
Victoria M. Sackville-West

Do not change Arthur George Rust, Jr., to Arthur George Rust, for example, or drop the hyphen in Victoria M. Sackville-West. In subsequent uses, you may refer to a person by his or her family name only (unless, of course, you refer to two or more persons with the same family name).

*see sec. 1.1.4*

Family names are treated differently in different languages. In some languages (e.g., Chinese, Hungarian, Japanese, Korean, and Vietnamese), family names precede given names.

### 1.1.2 Titles of Authors

If the name of the author of a source you consulted is given in the source with a title—such as *Dr.*, *Saint*, or *Sir*—generally omit the title in the works-cited list. Similarly, a title should usually not be included when the name is mentioned in the text discussion.

Augustine (not Saint Augustine)
Samuel Johnson (not Dr. Johnson)
Philip Sidney (not Sir Philip Sidney)

### 1.1.3 Names of Authors and Fictional Characters

It is common and acceptable to use simplified names of famous authors.

Dante (Dante Alighieri)
Virgil (Publius Vergilius Maro)

Pseudonyms in the works-cited list *see sec. 2.1.1*

Also acceptable are pseudonyms of authors.

Molière (Jean-Baptiste Poquelin)
George Eliot (Mary Ann Evans)
Mark Twain (Samuel Clemens)

Refer to fictional characters in your text in the same way that the work of fiction does. You need not always use their full names, and you may retain titles as appropriate (Dr. Jekyll, Madame Defarge).

## 1.1.4 Names in Languages Other Than English

### *Asian Languages*

The name of the author of a work published in Chinese, Japanese, Korean, or Vietnamese probably appears on the publication with the family name first. If so, in the works-cited list the author's name should be given in that order and not reversed. Since the name is not reversed, no comma is added to it. When the author of a work in English has a Chinese, Japanese, Korean, or Vietnamese name, the name might appear on the publication with the family name first or last. Determine which part is the family name, and reverse the author's name in the works-cited list only if the family name is not first. The following examples are names of writers as they might appear in the source.

Gao Xingjian (family name first)
Kenzaburō Ōe (family name last)

This is how they would appear in the list of works cited.

Gao Xingjian
Ōe, Kenzaburō

And this is how they would appear in a text discussion after the initial use of the full name.

Gao
Ōe

In an English-language context, names of persons, places, and organizations in Asian languages are romanized—spelled in the Latin alphabet as they are pronounced. Various systems of romanization have been devised for most of these languages. For example, the Wade-Giles system was once widely used for Chinese, but pinyin, the official romanization system in mainland China, is now standard among English speakers. In your sources, you may find the same Chinese names written in both systems—for instance, Mao Tse-tung (Wade-Giles) and Mao Zedong (pinyin). The pinyin forms are preferable, but the names of a few historical figures remain better known in older spellings, which may appear in reference works (e.g., Lao-tzu, Li Po). If you are uncertain how to romanize terms in a particular language, ask your instructor or consult *The Chicago Manual of Style* or *ALA-LC Romanization Tables*.

*ALA-LC Romanization Tables*, loc.gov/catdir/cpso/roman.html.

### *French*

French *de* following a first name or a title such as *Mme* or *duc* is usually not treated as part of the last name.

La Boétie, Étienne de
Maupassant, Guy de
Nemours, Louis-Charles d'Orléans, duc de

When the last name has only one syllable, however, *de* is usually retained.

de Gaulle, Charles

The preposition also remains, in the form *d'*, when it elides with a last name beginning with a vowel.

d'Arcy, Pierre

The forms *du* and *des*—combinations of *de* with *le* and *les*—are always used with last names and are capitalized.

Des Périers, Bonaventure
Du Bos, Charles

In English-language contexts, *de* is often treated as part of the last name.

De Quincey, Thomas

### *German*

German *von* is generally not treated as part of the last name.

Droste-Hülshoff, Annette von
Kleist, Heinrich von

Some exceptions exist, especially in English-language contexts.

Von Braun, Wernher
Von Trapp, Maria

### *Italian*

The names of many Italians who lived before or during the Renaissance are alphabetized by first name.

Dante Alighieri

But other names of the period follow the standard practice.

Boccaccio, Giovanni

The names of members of historic families are also usually alphabetized by last name.

Medici, Lorenzo de'

In modern times, Italian *da*, *de*, *del*, *della*, *di*, and *d'* are usually capitalized and treated as part of the last name.

D'Annunzio, Gabriele
Da Ponte, Lorenzo
Del Buono, Oreste
Della Robbia, Andrea
De Sica, Vittorio
Di Costanzo, Angelo

### *Latin*

Use the forms of Roman names most common in English. You may include the full name in a parenthesis in the works-cited list.

Cicero (Marcus Tullius Cicero)
Horace (Quintus Horatius Flaccus)
Julius Caesar (Gaius Julius Caesar)
Livy (Titus Livius)
Ovid (Publius Ovidius Naso)
Virgil (Publius Vergilius Maro)

Some medieval and Renaissance figures are best known by their adopted or assigned Latin names.

Albertus Magnus (Albert von Bollstädt)
Copernicus (Mikołaj Kopernik)

***Spanish***

Spanish *de* is usually not treated as part of the last name.

Madariaga, Salvador de
Rueda, Lope de
Timoneda, Juan de

Spanish *del*, however, which is formed from the fusion of the preposition *de* and the definite article *el*, is capitalized and used with the last name.

Del Río, Ángel

A Spanish surname may include both the paternal name and the maternal name, with or without the conjunction *y*. The surname of a married woman usually includes her paternal surname and her husband's paternal surname, connected by *de*. Consult a biographical dictionary for guidance in distinguishing surnames and given names.

Carreño de Miranda, Juan
Cervantes Saavedra, Miguel de
Díaz del Castillo, Bernal
García Márquez, Gabriel
Larra y Sánchez de Castro, Mariano José
López de Ayala, Pero
Matute, Ana María
Ortega y Gasset, José
Quevedo y Villegas, Francisco Gómez de
Sinués de Marco, María del Pilar
Zayas y Sotomayor, María de

Authors commonly known by the maternal portions of their surnames, such as Galdós and Lorca, should nonetheless be alphabetized by their full surnames.

García Lorca, Federico
Pérez Galdós, Benito

## 1.2 Titles of Sources

Whenever you use the title of a source in your writing, take the title from an authoritative location in the work, not, for example, from the cover or the top of a page. Copy the title without reproducing any unusual typography, such as special capitalization or lowercasing of all letters.

see pp. 14–18

### 1.2.1 Capitalization and Punctuation

When you copy an English title or subtitle, capitalize the first word, the last word, and all principal words, including those that follow hyphens in compound terms. Therefore, capitalize the following parts of speech:

- Nouns (e.g., *flowers*, as in *The Flowers of Europe*)
- Pronouns (e.g., *our*, as in *Save Our Children*; *it*, as in *Some Like It Hot*)
- Verbs (e.g., *watches*, as in *America Watches Television*; *is*, as in *What Is Literature?*)
- Adjectives (e.g., *ugly*, as in *The Ugly Duckling*)
- Adverbs (e.g., *slightly*, as in *Only Slightly Corrupt*; *down*, as in *Go Down, Moses*)
- Subordinating conjunctions (e.g., *after, although, as if, as soon as, because, before, if, that, unless, until, when, where, while*, as in *One If by Land*)

Do not capitalize the following parts of speech when they fall in the middle of a title:

- Articles (*a*, *an*, *the*, as in *Under the Bamboo Tree*)
- Prepositions (e.g., *against*, *as*, *between*, *in*, *of*, *to*, as in *The Merchant of Venice* and "A Dialogue between the Soul and Body")
- Coordinating conjunctions (*and*, *but*, *for*, *nor*, *or*, *so*, *yet*, as in *Romeo and Juliet*)
- The *to* in infinitives (as in *How to Play Chess*)

Capitalize quotations in titles according to the guidelines above.

> "'I'm Ready for My Close-Up': Lloyd Webber on Screen"

see p. 29

When an untitled poem is known by its first line or when a short untitled message is identified in the works-cited list by its full text, the line or full text is reproduced exactly as it appears in the source.

> Dickinson's poem "I heard a Fly buzz—when I died—" contrasts the everyday and the momentous.

Use a colon and a space to separate a title from a subtitle, unless the title ends in a question mark or an exclamation point. Include other punctuation only if it is part of the title or subtitle.

*Storytelling and Mythmaking: Images from Film and Literature*
*Whose Music? A Sociology of Musical Language*

The following examples illustrate how to capitalize and punctuate a variety of titles:

*The Teaching of Spanish in English-Speaking Countries*
*Life As I Find It* (Here *as* is a subordinating conjunction.)
*The Artist as Critic* (Here *as* is a preposition.)
"Italian Literature before Dante"
"What Americans Stand For"
"Why Fortinbras?"
"Marcel Proust: Archetypal Music—an Exercise in Transcendence"

## 1.2.2 Italics and Quotation Marks

Handling titles within titles see sec. 1.2.4

Most titles should be italicized or enclosed in quotation marks. In general, italicize the titles of sources that are self-contained and independent (e.g., books) and the titles of containers (e.g., anthologies); use quotation marks for the titles of sources that are contained in larger works (e.g., short stories).

*The Awakening* (book)
*The Metamorphosis* (novella)
"Literary History and Sociology" (journal article)
*Stanford Encyclopedia of Philosophy* (Web site)
"Free Will" (article on a Web site)

This convention has a few exceptions. Names in the following categories are capitalized like titles but are not italicized or enclosed in quotation marks.

**Scripture**

Bible
Old Testament
Genesis
Gospels
Talmud
Koran *or* Quran *or* Qur'an
Upanishads

Titles of individual published editions of scriptural writings, however, should be italicized and treated like any other published work.

*The Interlinear Bible*
*The Talmud of the Land of Israel: A Preliminary Translation and Explanation*
*The Upanishads: A Selection for the Modern Reader*

**Laws, Acts, and Similar Political Documents**

Magna Carta
Declaration of Independence
Bill of Rights
Treaty of Trianon

**Musical Compositions Identified by Form, Number, and Key**

Beethoven's Symphony no. 7 in A, op. 92
Vivaldi's Concerto for Two Trumpets and Strings in C, RV539

**Series**

Critical American Studies
Bollingen Series

**Conferences, Seminars, Workshops, and Courses**

International Symposium on Cultural Diplomacy 2015
Introduction to Calculus
Anthropology 102
Geographic Information Analysis Workshop
MLA Annual Convention

Words designating the divisions of a work are also not italicized or put in quotation marks, nor are they capitalized when used in the text ("The author says in her preface . . . ," "In canto 32 Ariosto writes . . .").

| | |
|---|---|
| preface | chapter 2 |
| introduction | bibliography |
| list of works cited | canto 32 |
| appendix | act 4 |
| scene 7 | index |
| stanza 20 | |

### 1.2.3 Shortened Titles

When you refer to a title in your discussion, state the title in full, though you may omit a nonessential subtitle. If you refer to a title often in your discussion, you may, after stating the title in full at least once, use an abbreviation, preferably a familiar or obvious one (e.g., "Nightingale" for "Ode to a Nightingale"). If the abbreviation may not be clear on its own, introduce it in a parenthesis when the title is first given in full: "In *All's Well That Ends Well* (*AWW*), Shakespeare. . . ."

Abbreviating titles in in-text citations *see sec. 3.2.1*

It is common in legal scholarship to refer to a law case by the first nongovernmental party. For instance, when commenting on a case named *NLRB v. Yeshiva University* (involving the National Labor Relations Board, a federal agency), scholars are likely to use *Yeshiva* as a short title. But in MLA style, readers need the first part of the name (*NLRB*) to locate the full citation in the list of works cited. Thus, if you follow the standard practice of using *Yeshiva* in your text discussion, you will need to include *NLRB* in your parenthetical citation.

### 1.2.4 Titles within Titles

Italicize a title normally indicated by italics when it appears within a title enclosed in quotation marks.

"*Romeo and Juliet* and Renaissance Politics" (an article about a play)

"Language and Childbirth in *The Awakening*" (an article about a novel)

When a title normally indicated by quotation marks appears within another title requiring quotation marks, enclose the inner title in single quotation marks.

"Lines after Reading 'Sailing to Byzantium'" (a poem about a poem)

"The Uncanny Theology of 'A Good Man Is Hard to Find'" (an article about a short story)

Use quotation marks around a title normally indicated by quotation marks when it appears within an italicized title.

*"The Lottery" and Other Stories* (a book of stories)

*New Perspectives on "The Eve of St. Agnes"* (a book about a poem)

If a period is required after an italicized title that ends with a quotation mark, place the period before the quotation mark.

The study appears in *New Perspectives on "The Eve of St. Agnes."*

When a normally italicized title appears within another italicized title, the title within is neither italicized nor enclosed in quotation marks; it is in roman.

*Approaches to Teaching Murasaki Shikibu's* The Tale of Genji (a book about a novel)

*From* The Lodger *to* The Lady Vanishes*: Hitchcock's Classic British Thrillers* (a book about films)

## 1.2.5 Titles of Sources in Languages Other Than English

If your readers are unlikely to understand the title of a non-English-language work in your text discussion, provide a translation in a parenthesis.

Translations of titles in the works-cited list *see sec. 2.2.2*

> Isabel Allende based her novel *La casa de los espíritus* (*The House of the Spirits*) on a letter she had written to her dying grandfather.

### *French*

In prose and verse, French capitalization is the same as English except that the following terms are not capitalized in French unless they begin sentences or, sometimes, lines of verse: (1) the subject pronoun *je* ("I"), (2) the names of months and days of the week, (3) the names of languages, (4) adjectives derived from proper nouns, (5) titles preceding personal names, and (6) the words meaning "street," "square," "lake," "mountain," and so on, in most place-names.

In a title or a subtitle, capitalize only the first word and all words normally capitalized.

> *La chambre claire: Note sur la photographie*
> *Du côté de chez Swann*
> *La guerre de Troie n'aura pas lieu*
> *Nouvelle revue d'onomastique*

### *German*

In German capitalize all nouns—including adjectives, infinitives, pronouns, prepositions, and other parts of speech used as nouns—as well as the pronoun *Sie* ("you") and its possessive, *Ihr* ("your"), and their inflected forms. The following terms are generally not capitalized unless they begin sentences or, usually, lines of verse: (1) the subject pronoun *ich* ("I"), (2) the names of languages and of days of the week used as adjectives, adverbs, or complements of prepositions, and (3) adjectives and adverbs formed from proper nouns, except when the proper nouns are names of persons and the adjectives and adverbs refer to the persons' works or deeds.

In a title or a subtitle, capitalize only the first word and all words normally capitalized.

*Lethe: Kunst und Kritik des Vergessens*
*Ein treuer Diener seines Herrn*
*Zeitschrift für vergleichende Sprachforschung*

### *Italian*

In prose and verse, Italian capitalization is the same as English except that in Italian, centuries and other large divisions of time are capitalized (*il Seicento*) and the following terms are not capitalized unless they begin sentences or, usually, lines of verse: (1) the subject pronoun *io* ("I"), (2) the names of months and days of the week, (3) the names of languages and nationalities, (4) nouns, adjectives, and adverbs derived from proper nouns, (5) titles preceding personal names, and (6) the words meaning "street," "square," and so on, in most place names.

In a title or a subtitle, capitalize only the first word and all words normally capitalized.

*L'arte tipografica in Urbino*
*Bibliografia della critica pirandelliana*
*Collezione di classici italiani*
*Luigi Pulci e la Chimera: Studi sull'allegoria nel* Morgante
*Studi petrarcheschi*

### *Latin*

Although practice varies, Latin most commonly follows the English rules for capitalization, except that *ego* ("I") is not capitalized. In the title or subtitle of a classical or medieval work, however, capitalize only the first word and all words normally capitalized.

*De senectute*
*Pro Marcello*

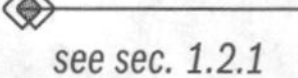

see sec. 1.2.1

Titles of postmedieval works in Latin are often capitalized like English titles.

> *Tractatus de Intellectus Emendatione*

### *Spanish*

In prose and verse, Spanish capitalization is the same as English except that the following terms are not capitalized in Spanish unless they begin sentences or, sometimes, lines of verse: (1) the subject pronoun *yo* ("I"), (2) the names of months and days of the week, (3) the names of languages and nationalities, (4) nouns and adjectives derived from proper nouns, (5) titles preceding personal names, and (6) the words meaning "street," "square," and so on, in most place-names.

In a title or a subtitle, capitalize only the first word and all words normally capitalized.

> *Breve historia del ensayo hispanoamericano*
> *Cortejo a lo prohibido: Lectoras y escritoras en la España moderna*
> *Extremos de América*
> *La gloria de don Ramiro*
> *Historia verdadera de la conquista de la Nueva España*
> *Revista de filología española*

### *Romanized Languages*

see sec. 1.3.8

If you discuss works in a language not written in the Latin alphabet (e.g., Arabic, Chinese, Greek, Hebrew, Japanese, Russian), give their titles and quotations from them consistently in the original writing system or in romanization. In a romanized title or subtitle, capitalize the first word and any words that would be capitalized in English prose.

> ثرثرة فوق النيل (*Adrift on the Nile*)

or

> *Thartharah fawqa al-Nīl* (*Adrift on the Nile*)

If you are uncertain how to romanize terms in a particular language, ask your instructor or consult *The Chicago Manual of Style* or *ALA-LC Romanization Tables*.

*Other Languages*

When you copy a title or a subtitle in nearly any language using the Latin alphabet not discussed above, it is appropriate to capitalize only the first word and all words capitalized in regular prose in the same work.

## 1.3 Quotations

### 1.3.1 Use and Accuracy of Quotations

Quotations are most effective in research writing when used selectively. Quote only words, phrases, lines, and passages that are particularly apt, and keep all quotations as brief as possible. Your project should be about your own ideas, and quotations should merely help you explain or illustrate them.

The accuracy of quotations is crucial. They must reproduce the original sources exactly. Unless indicated in square brackets or parentheses, changes must not be made in the spelling, capitalization, or interior punctuation of the source. You must construct a clear, grammatically correct sentence that allows you to introduce or incorporate a quotation with complete accuracy. Alternatively, you may paraphrase the original and quote only fragments, which may be easier to integrate into the flow of your writing. If you change a quotation in any way, make the alteration clear to the reader by following the rules and recommendations below.

see sec. 1.3.6

### 1.3.2 Prose

If a prose quotation runs no more than four lines and requires no special emphasis, put it in quotation marks and incorporate it into the text.

> "It was the best of times, it was the worst of times," wrote Charles Dickens of the eighteenth century.

The sample sentences so far in this section include quotations but don't end with citations. Not every sentence with borrowed material has to contain a citation. If you draw repeatedly from a source without referring to another one, you can often wait to provide the citations until you're done using the source in your text (see sec. 3.5). Some sources (especially online publications) lack page numbers or fixed part numbers and so offer no numbers to be cited.

You need not always reproduce complete sentences. Sometimes you may want to quote just a word or phrase as part of your sentence.

> For Charles Dickens the eighteenth century was both "the best of times" and "the worst of times."

You may put a quotation at the beginning, middle, or end of your sentence or, for the sake of variety or better style, divide it by your own words.

> Joseph Conrad writes of the company manager in *Heart of Darkness*, "He was obeyed, yet he inspired neither love nor fear, nor even respect."

or

> "He was obeyed," writes Joseph Conrad of the company manager in *Heart of Darkness*, "yet he inspired neither love nor fear, nor even respect."

Punctuation with quotations *see sec. 1.3.7*

If a quotation ending a sentence requires a parenthetical reference, place the sentence period after the reference.

> For Charles Dickens the eighteenth century was both "the best of times" and "the worst of times" (35).
>
> "He was obeyed," writes Joseph Conrad of the company manager in *Heart of Darkness*, "yet he inspired neither love nor fear, nor even respect" (87).

If a quotation extends to more than four lines when run into your text, set it off from the text as a block indented half an inch from the left margin. Do not indent the first line an extra amount or add quotation marks not present in the original. A colon introduces a quotation displayed in this way except when the grammatical connection between your introductory wording and the quotation requires a different mark of punctuation or none at all. A parenthetical reference for a prose quotation set off from the text follows the last line of the quotation.

> At the conclusion of *Lord of the Flies*, Ralph, realizing the horror of his actions, is overcome by
>
> > great, shuddering spasms of grief that seemed to wrench his whole body. His voice rose under the black smoke before the burning wreckage of the island; and infected by that emotion, the other little boys began to shake and sob too. (186)

If a new paragraph begins in the middle of the quotation, indent its first line.

> In *Moll Flanders* Defoe follows the picaresque tradition by using a pseudoautobiographical narration:
>
> > My true name is so well known in the records, or registers, at Newgate and in the Old Bailey, and there are some things of such consequence still depending there relating to my particular conduct, that it is not to be expected I should set my name or the account of my family to this work. . . .
> >
> > It is enough to tell you, that . . . some of my worst comrades, who are out of the way of doing me harm . . . know me by the name of Moll Flanders. . . . (1)

Ellipses in quotations *see sec. 1.3.5*

### 1.3.3 Poetry

If you quote part or all of a line of verse that does not require special emphasis, put it in quotation marks within your text, just as you would a line of prose. You may also incorporate two or three lines in this way, using a forward slash with a space on each side ( / ) to indicate to your reader where the line breaks fall.

> Bradstreet frames the poem with a sense of mortality: "All things within this fading world hath end. . . ."

> Reflecting on the "incident" in Baltimore, Cullen concludes, "Of all the things that happened there / That's all that I remember."

If a stanza break occurs in the quotation, mark it with two forward slashes ( // ).

> The *Tao te ching*, in David Hinton's translation, says that the ancient masters were "so deep beyond knowing / we can only describe their appearance: // perfectly cautious, as if crossing winter streams. . . . "

In-text citations for verse *see sec. 3.3.2*

Verse quotations of more than three lines should be set off from your text as a block. Unless the quotation involves unusual spacing, indent it half an inch from the left margin. Do not add quotation marks not present in the original. A verse quotation may require citing line and other division numbers, a page number, or no number, depending on its length and whether it is published in editions with numbered lines. The in-text citation for a verse quotation set off from the text in this way, if required, follows the last line of the quotation (as it does with prose quotations). If the citation will not fit on the same line as the end of the quotation, it should appear on a new line, flush with the right margin of the page.

> In Walt Whitman's "When Lilacs Last in the Dooryard Bloom'd," the poet's gaze sweeps across the nation from east to west like the sun:
>
> > Lo, body and soul—this land,
> > My own Manhattan with spires, and the sparkling and hurrying tides, and the ships,
> > The varied and ample land, the South and the North in the light, Ohio's shores and flashing Missouri,
> > And ever the far-spreading prairies cover'd with grass and corn. (canto 12)

A line too long to fit within the right margin should be formatted with hanging indention, so that its continuation is indented more than the rest of the block.

If the layout of the lines in the original text, including indention and spacing within and between them, is unusual, reproduce it as accurately as possible.

> E. E. Cummings concludes the poem with this vivid description of a carefree scene, reinforced by the carefree form of the lines themselves:
>
> it's<br>
> spring<br>
> and<br>
>         the<br>
> <br>
>                goat-footed<br>
> <br>
> balloonMan        whistles<br>
> far<br>
> and<br>
> wee (16-24)

When a verse quotation begins in the middle of a line, the partial line should be positioned where it is in the original and not shifted to the left margin.

> In "I Sit and Sew," by Alice Dunbar-Nelson, the speaker laments that social convention compels her to sit uselessly while her male compatriots lie in need on the battlefield:
>
>                My soul in pity flings<br>
> Appealing cries, yearning only to go<br>
> There in that holocaust of hell, those fields of woe—<br>
> But—I must sit and sew.

### 1.3.4 Drama

If you quote dialogue in a play or screenplay, set the quotation off from your text. Begin each part of the dialogue with the appropriate character's name, indented half an inch from the left margin and written in all capital letters: HAMLET. Follow the name with a period and then start the quotation. Indent all subsequent lines in that character's speech an additional amount. When the dialogue shifts to another character, start a new line indented half an inch. Maintain this pattern throughout the entire quotation.

> Marguerite Duras's screenplay for *Hiroshima mon amour* suggests at the outset the profound difference between observation and experience:
>
> > HE. You saw nothing in Hiroshima. Nothing. . . .
> > SHE. I saw *everything. Everything.* . . . The hospital, for
> > instance, I saw it. I'm sure I did. There is a hospital
> > in Hiroshima. How could I help seeing it? . . .
> > HE. You did not see the hospital in Hiroshima. You saw
> > nothing in Hiroshima. (15-17)

> A short time later Lear loses the final symbol of his former power, the soldiers who make up his train:
>
> > GONERIL. Hear me, my lord.
> > What need you five-and-twenty, ten or five,
> > To follow in a house where twice so many
> > Have a command to tend you?
> > REGAN. What need one?
> > LEAR. O, reason not the need! (2.4.254-58)

### 1.3.5 Ellipsis

Whenever you omit a word, a phrase, a sentence, or more from a quoted passage, you should be guided by two principles: fairness to the author quoted and the grammatical integrity of your writing. A quotation should never be presented in a way that could cause a reader to misunderstand the sentence structure of the original source. If the fact that you omitted material from a sentence or series of sentences is not obvious, you must mark the omission with ellipsis points, or three spaced periods. When you quote only a word or phrase, no ellipsis points are needed before or after the quotation because it is obvious that you left out some of the original sentence.

> In his inaugural address, John F. Kennedy spoke of a "new frontier."

When your quotation reads like a complete sentence, however, an ellipsis is needed at the end if the original sentence does not end there, as the following examples show. An omission in the middle of a quotation always requires an ellipsis. Whenever you omit words from a quotation, the resulting passage—your prose and the quotation integrated into it—should be grammatically complete and correct.

#### *Omission within a Sentence*

Identify an omission within a sentence by using three periods with a space before each and a space after the last ( . . . ).

**Original**

> Medical thinking, trapped in the theory of astral influences, stressed air as the communicator of disease, ignoring sanitation or visible carriers.
>
> From Barbara W. Tuchman's *A Distant Mirror: The Calamitous Fourteenth Century* (Ballantine, 1979)

**Quotation with an Ellipsis in the Middle**

> In surveying various responses to plagues in the Middle Ages, Barbara W. Tuchman writes, "Medical thinking . . . stressed air as the communicator of disease, ignoring sanitation or visible carriers" (101-02).

When the ellipsis coincides with the end of your sentence, place a period after the last word of the quotation and then add three periods with a space before each.

**Quotation with an Ellipsis at the End**

In surveying various responses to plagues in the Middle Ages, Barbara W. Tuchman writes, "Medical thinking, trapped in the theory of astral influences, stressed air as the communicator of disease. . . ."

If a parenthetical reference follows the ellipsis at the end of your sentence, use three periods with a space before each, and place the sentence period after the final parenthesis.

**Quotation with an Ellipsis at the End Followed by a Parenthetical Reference**

In surveying various responses to plagues in the Middle Ages, Barbara W. Tuchman writes, "Medical thinking, trapped in the theory of astral influences, stressed air as the communicator of disease . . ." (101-02).

### *Omission in a Quotation of More Than One Sentence*

An ellipsis in the middle of a quotation can indicate the omission of any amount of text.

**Original**

Presidential control reached its zenith under Andrew Jackson, the extent of whose attention to the press even before he became a candidate is suggested by the fact that he subscribed to twenty newspapers. Jackson was never content to have only one organ grinding out his tune. For a time, the *United States Telegraph* and the *Washington Globe* were almost equally favored as party organs, and there were fifty-seven journalists on the government payroll.

From William L. Rivers's *The Mass Media: Reporting, Writing, Editing* (2nd ed., Harper and Row, 1975)

### Quotation Omitting a Sentence

In discussing the historical relation between politics and the press, William L. Rivers notes:

> Presidential control reached its zenith under Andrew Jackson, the extent of whose attention to the press even before he became a candidate is suggested by the fact that he subscribed to twenty newspapers. . . . For a time, the *United States Telegraph* and the *Washington Globe* were almost equally favored as party organs, and there were fifty-seven journalists on the government payroll. (7)

### Quotation with an Omission from the Middle of One Sentence to the End of Another

In discussing the historical relation between politics and the press, William L. Rivers notes, "Presidential control reached its zenith under Andrew Jackson. . . . For a time, the *United States Telegraph* and the *Washington Globe* were almost equally favored as party organs, and there were fifty-seven journalists on the government payroll" (7).

By convention, the period that marks the end of the sentence beginning "Presidential control" in the above example is placed before the ellipsis.

### Quotation with an Omission from the Middle of One Sentence to the Middle of Another

In discussing the historical relation between politics and the press, William L. Rivers notes that when presidential control "reached its zenith under Andrew Jackson, . . . there were fifty-seven journalists on the government payroll" (7).

### *Omission in a Quotation of Poetry*

Use three or four spaced periods in quotations of poetry, as in quotations of prose.

### Original

In Worcester, Massachusetts,
I went with Aunt Consuelo
to keep her dentist's appointment
and sat and waited for her
in the dentist's waiting room.
It was winter. It got dark
early. The waiting room
was full of grown-up people,
arctics and overcoats,
lamps and magazines.

From Elizabeth Bishop's "In the Waiting Room" (*Poets.org*, Academy of American Poets, www.poets.org/poetsorg/poem/waiting-room)

### Quotation with an Ellipsis at the End

Elizabeth Bishop's "In the Waiting Room" is rich in evocative detail:

In Worcester, Massachusetts,
I went with Aunt Consuelo
to keep her dentist's appointment
and sat and waited for her
in the dentist's waiting room.
It was winter. It got dark
early. The waiting room
was full of grown-up people. . . .

An ellipsis is needed in this example because without it the reader would think that "people" was the last word of the original sentence.

The omission of a line or more in the middle of a poetry quotation that is set off from the text is indicated by a line of spaced periods approximately the length of a complete line of the quoted poem.

**Quotation Omitting a Line or More in the Middle**

Elizabeth Bishop's "In the Waiting Room" is rich in evocative detail:

In Worcester, Massachusetts,
I went with Aunt Consuelo
to keep her dentist's appointment
. . . . . . . . . . . . . . . . . . . . . . . . .
It was winter. It got dark
early.

In this example, no ellipsis is needed at the end because "early" is the last word of the original sentence. The reader will not misunderstand the poem's sentence structure. You do not need to indicate that more material appears on the line in the original.

### *An Ellipsis in the Source*

If the author you are quoting uses ellipsis points, you should distinguish them from your ellipses by putting square brackets around the ones you add or by including an explanatory phrase in a parenthesis after the quotation.

**Original**

"We live in California, my husband and I, Los Angeles. . . . This is beautiful country; I have never been here before."

From N. Scott Momaday's *House Made of Dawn* (Harper and Row, 1977)

**Quotation with an Added Ellipsis**

In N. Scott Momaday's *House Made of Dawn*, when Mrs. St. John arrives at the rectory, she tells Father Olguin, "We live in California, my husband and I, Los Angeles. . . . This is beautiful country [. . .]" (29).

or

In N. Scott Momaday's *House Made of Dawn*, when Mrs. St. John arrives at the rectory, she tells Father Olguin, "We live in California, my husband and I, Los Angeles. . . . This is beautiful country . . ." (29; 1st ellipsis in original).

## 1.3.6 Other Alterations of Quotations

Occasionally, you may decide that a quotation will be unclear or confusing to your reader unless you provide supplementary information. For example, you may need to insert material missing from the original or add "sic" (an English word—hence not italicized—from the Latin for "thus" or "so") to assure readers that the quotation is accurate even though the spelling or logic might make them think otherwise. You may also italicize words for emphasis. Keep such alterations to a minimum and distinguish them from the original.

A comment or an explanation that immediately follows the closing quotation mark appears in a parenthesis.

> Shaw admitted, "Nothing can extinguish my interest in Shakespear" (sic).
>
> Lincoln specifically advocated a government "*for* the people" (emphasis added).

A comment or an explanation that goes inside the quotation must appear within square brackets.

> He claimed he could provide "hundreds of examples [of court decisions] to illustrate the historical tension between church and state."
>
> Milton's Satan speaks of his "study [pursuit] of revenge."

Similarly, if a pronoun in a quotation seems unclear, you may add an identification in square brackets.

> In the first act he soliloquizes, "Why, she would hang on him [Hamlet's father] / As if increase of appetite had grown / By what it fed on. . . ."

### 1.3.7 Punctuation with Quotations

Whether incorporated into or set off from the text, quoted material is usually preceded by a colon if the quotation is formally introduced and by a comma or no punctuation if the quotation is an integral part of the sentence structure.

> Shelley held a bold view: "Poets are the unacknowledged legislators of the World" (794).
>
> "Poets," according to Shelley, "are the unacknowledged legislators of the World" (794).
>
> Shelley thought poets "the unacknowledged legislators of the World" (794).

Do not use opening and closing quotation marks to enclose quotations set off from the text, but reproduce any quotation marks that are in the passage quoted.

> In "Memories of West Street and Lepke," Robert Lowell, a conscientious objector (or "C.O."), recounts meeting a Jehovah's Witness in prison:
>
> > I was so out of things, I'd never heard<br>
> > of the Jehovah's Witnesses.<br>
> > "Are you a C.O.?" I asked a fellow jailbird.<br>
> > "No," he answered, "I'm a J.W." (36-39)

Use double quotation marks around quotations incorporated into the text and single quotation marks around quotations within those quotations.

> In "Memories of West Street and Lepke," Robert Lowell, a conscientious objector (or "C.O."), recounts meeting a Jehovah's Witness in prison: "'Are you a C.O.?' I asked a fellow jailbird. / 'No,' he answered, 'I'm a J.W.'" (38-39).

When a quotation consists entirely of material enclosed by quotation marks in the source work, usually one pair of double quotation marks is sufficient, provided that the introductory wording makes clear the special character of the quoted material.

> Meeting a fellow prisoner, Lowell asks, "Are you a C.O.?" (38).

Except for changing internal double quotation marks to single ones when you incorporate quotations into your text, you should reproduce internal punctuation exactly as in the original. The closing punctuation, though, depends on where the quoted material appears in your sentence. Suppose, for example, that you want to quote the following sentence: "You've got to be carefully taught." If you begin your sentence with this line, you need to replace the closing period with a punctuation mark appropriate to the new context.

> "You've got to be carefully taught," wrote Oscar Hammerstein II about how racial prejudice is perpetuated.

If the quotation ends with a question mark or an exclamation point, however, the original punctuation is retained, and no comma is required.

Preserving original spelling *see sec. 1.3.1*

> "How can I describe my emotions at this catastrophe, or how delineate the wretch whom with such infinite pains and care I had endeavoured to form?" wonders Victor Frankenstein in Mary Shelley's *Frankenstein* (42).

> "What a wonderful little almanac you are, Celia!" Dorothea Brooke responds to her sister (7).

By convention, commas and periods that directly follow quotations go inside the closing quotation marks. When a quotation is directly followed by a parenthetical citation, however, any required comma or period follows the citation.

Thus, if a quotation ends with a period and falls at the end of your sentence, the period appears after the reference.

> N. Scott Momaday's *House Made of Dawn* begins with an image that also concludes the novel: "Abel was running" (7).

If a quotation ends with both single and double quotation marks, the comma or period precedes both.

> "The poem alludes to Stevens's 'Sunday Morning,'" notes Miller.

All other punctuation marks—such as semicolons, colons, question marks, and exclamation points—go outside a closing quotation mark, except when they are part of the quoted material.

**Original**

> Have you felt so proud to get at the meaning of poems?
>
> From Walt Whitman's "Song of Myself," in *Leaves of Grass* (McKay, 1892)

**Quotations**

> Whitman refers to "the meaning of poems."
>
> Where does Whitman refer to "the meaning of poems"?

but

> Whitman asks, "Have you felt so proud to get at the meaning of poems?"

If a quotation ending with a question mark or an exclamation point concludes your sentence and requires a parenthetical reference, retain the original punctuation within the quotation mark and follow with the reference and the sentence period outside the quotation mark.

> In Mary Shelley's *Frankenstein*, Victor Frankenstein wonders, "How can I describe my emotions at this catastrophe, or how

delineate the wretch whom with such infinite pains and care I had endeavoured to form?" (42).

Dorothea Brooke responds to her sister, "What a wonderful little almanac you are, Celia!" (7).

## 1.3.8 Translations of Quotations

If you believe that a significant portion of your audience will not understand the language of a quotation you present, you should add a translation. Give the source of the translation in addition to the source of the quotation. In general, the translation should immediately follow the quotation whether the two passages are incorporated into or set off from the text, although the order may be reversed if it is unlikely that readers will be able to read the original. If the pair of passages are incorporated into the text, distinguish them from each other by placing the second one in double quotation marks and parentheses or in single quotation marks and not in parentheses. Separate elements in parentheses with semicolons.

At the opening of Dante's *Inferno*, the poet finds himself in "una selva oscura" ("a dark wood"; 1.2; Ciardi 28).

Citing verse by division numbers *see sec. 3.3.2*

or

At the opening of Dante's *Inferno*, the poet finds himself in "una selva oscura" 'a dark wood' (1.2; Ciardi 28).

If you created the translation, insert *my trans.* in place of a source in the parenthetical citation.

Sévigné responds to praise of her much admired letters by acknowledging that "there is nothing stiff about them" ("pour figées, elles ne le sont pas"; my trans.; 489).

or

Sévigné responds to praise of her much admired letters by acknowledging that "there is nothing stiff about them" 'pour figées, elles ne le sont pas' (my trans.; 489).

If your project includes many translations that you created, it may be more convenient to introduce an endnote describing which translations are yours. The endnote would be located immediately after your first translation. Then *my trans.* would not appear after any translation covered by the note.

Do not use quotation marks around quotations and translations set off from the text.

> Dante's *Inferno* begins literally in the middle of things:
>
> Nel mezzo del cammin di nostra vita
> mi ritrovai per una selva oscura,
> ché la diritta via era smarrita.
> Ahi quanto a dir qual era è cosa dura
> esta selva selvaggia e aspra e forte
> che nel pensier rinova la paura! (1.1-6)
> Midway in our life's journey, I went astray
> from the straight road and woke to find myself
> alone in a dark wood. How shall I say
> what wood that was! I never saw so drear,
> so rank, so arduous a wilderness!
> Its very memory gives a shape to fear. (Ciardi 28)

Quotations from works in a language not written in the Latin alphabet (e.g., Arabic, Chinese, Greek, Hebrew, Japanese, Russian), as well as the works' titles, should be given consistently in the original writing system or in romanization. Names of persons, places, and organizations, however, are usually romanized.

> As Chekhov's *The Cherry Orchard* (Вишнёвый сад) opens, Lopakhin remembers being called a "little peasant" ("мужичок") when he was a boy (4; 117-18; act 1).

> Genesis 6.4 looks back to an earlier state of society: ". . . הנפלים היו בארץ בימים ההם" 'There were giants in the earth in those days . . .' (*Bible Hub*).

## 1.4 Numbers

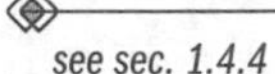
see sec. 1.4.4

Although there are a few well-established uses for roman numerals, numbers not spelled out are commonly represented by arabic numerals.

### 1.4.1 Use of Numerals or Words

In discussions that require few numbers, you may spell out numbers written in a word or two and represent other numbers by numerals (*one*, *thirty-six*, *ninety-nine*, *one hundred*, *fifteen hundred*, *two thousand*, *three million*, but *2½*, *101*, *137*, *1,275*). To form the plural of a spelled-out number, treat the word like an ordinary noun (*sixes*, *sevens*).

If your project calls for frequent use of numbers, use numerals for all numbers that precede technical units of measurement (*30 inches*, *5 kilograms*). In such a project, also use numerals for numbers that are presented together and that refer to similar things, such as in comparisons or reports of experimental data. Spell out other numbers if they can be written in one or two words. Large numbers may be expressed in a combination of numerals and words (*4.5 million*).

Use numerals with abbreviations or symbols (*6 lbs.*, *4:00 p.m.*, *$3.50*); in street addresses (*4401 13th Avenue*); in dates (*11 April 2006*); in decimal fractions (*8.3*); and for items in numbered series (*year 3*, *chapter 9*, *volume 1*—or, in documentation, *ch. 1* and *vol. 1*). When a numeral falls at the start of a sentence, either spell out the number (if doing so is not awkward) or revise the sentence to place the numeral later in it.

### 1.4.2 Commas in Numbers

Commas are usually placed between the third and fourth digits from the right, the sixth and seventh, and so on.

1,000
20,000
7,654,321

Commas are not used in page and line numbers, in street addresses, or in four-digit years.

### 1.4.3 Inclusive Numbers

In a range of numbers, give the second number in full for numbers up to ninety-nine.

| | |
|---|---|
| 2-3 | 21-48 |
| 10-12 | 89-99 |

For larger numbers, give only the last two digits of the second number, unless more are necessary for clarity.

| | |
|---|---|
| 96-101 | 923-1,003 |
| 103-04 | 1,003-05 |
| 395-401 | 1,608-774 |

In a range of years beginning AD 1000 or later, omit the first two digits of the second year if they are the same as the first two digits of the first year. Otherwise, write both years in full.

| | |
|---|---|
| 2000-03 | 1898-1901 |

In a range of years beginning from AD 1 through 999, follow the rules for inclusive numbers in general. Do not abbreviate ranges of years that begin before AD 1.

### 1.4.4 Roman Numerals

Use capital roman numerals for the primary divisions of an outline and as suffixes for the names of persons.

Elizabeth II

John D. Rockefeller IV

Use lowercase roman numerals for citing pages of a book that are so numbered (e.g., the pages in a preface). Write out inclusive roman numerals in full: *xxv–xxvi*, *xlvi–xlix*.

## 1.5 Dates and Times

In the body of your writing, do not abbreviate dates, and be consistent in your use of either the day-month-year style (*12 January 2014*) or the month-day-year style (*January 12, 2014*). In the latter style, the comma before the year has to be balanced by one after if there is no other punctuation after the year.

> October 28, 1466, is Erasmus's likely date of birth (Gleason 76).

In the list of works cited, use the day-month-year style (*12 Jan. 2014*) to minimize the number of commas. Months may be abbreviated. Dates in the works-cited list should be given as fully as they appear in your sources. When times are available, include them as well. Times should be expressed consistently in either the twelve-hour or the twenty-four-hour clock. Include time zone information when provided.

*see sec. 1.6.1*

Uncertain dates are usually indicated by a question mark.

> Dickinson, Emily. "Distance Is Not the Realm of Fox." 1870?, Pierpont Morgan Library, New York. Manuscript.

Dates that are only generally known may be described; use lowercase words rather than numerals to designate a century.

> Chaucer, Geoffrey. *The Canterbury Tales*. Early fifteenth century, Bodleian Library, Oxford, Corpus Christi College MS 198.

Though lowercase in the body of your writing, seasons of the year are capitalized when part of a publication date in the works-cited list.

> Belton, John. "Painting by the Numbers: The Digital Intermediate." *Film Quarterly*, vol. 61, no. 3, Spring 2008, pp. 58-65.

## 1.6 Abbreviations

Abbreviations are used regularly in the list of works cited and in in-text citations but rarely in the text of academic writing. If you use abbreviations, always choose accepted forms. While economy of space is important, clarity is more so. Spell out a term if the abbreviation may puzzle your readers.

Use neither periods after letters nor spaces between letters for abbreviations made up predominantly of capital letters.

| | | |
|---|---|---|
| BC | NJ | US |
| DVD | PhD | |

The chief exception is the initials used in the names of persons: a period and a space follow each initial unless the name is entirely reduced to initials.

| | |
|---|---|
| JFK | J. R. R. Tolkien |

Most abbreviations that end in lowercase letters are followed by periods.

| | | |
|---|---|---|
| ed. | pp. | vol. |

In most abbreviations made up of lowercase letters that each represent a word, a period follows each letter, but no space intervenes between letters.

| | | |
|---|---|---|
| a.m. | e.g. | i.e. |

### 1.6.1 Months

The names of months that are longer than four letters are abbreviated in the works-cited list.

| | | |
|---|---|---|
| Jan. | Apr. | Oct. |
| Feb. | Aug. | Nov. |
| Mar. | Sept. | Dec. |

## 1.6.2 Common Academic Abbreviations

The following abbreviations are recommended for use in the works-cited list and in in-text citations. Where confusion may result, spell out the words instead. The plurals of the noun abbreviations given here other than *p.* are formed through the addition of *s* (e.g., *chs.*).

| | |
|---|---|
| ch. | chapter |
| dept. | department |
| ed. | edition |
| e.g. | for example (from the Latin *exempli gratia*; set off by commas, unless preceded by a different punctuation mark) |
| et al. | and others (from the Latin *et alii*, *et aliae*, *et alia*) |
| etc. | and so forth (from the Latin *et cetera*; like most abbreviations, not appropriate in text) |
| i.e. | that is (from the Latin *id est*; set off by commas, unless preceded by a different punctuation mark) |
| no. | number |
| P | Press (used in documentation in names of academic presses: "MIT P") |
| p., pp. | page, pages |
| par. | paragraph |
| qtd. in | quoted in |
| rev. | revised |
| sec. | section |
| trans. | translation |
| U | University (also French *Université*, German *Universität*, Italian *Università*, Spanish *Universidad*, etc.; used in documentation: "U of Tennessee, Knoxville") |

| | |
|---|---|
| UP | University Press (used in documentation: "Columbia UP") |
| vol. | volume |

### 1.6.3 Publishers' Names

When you give publishers' names in the list of works cited, omit business words like *Company* (*Co.*), *Corporation* (*Corp.*), *Incorporated* (*Inc.*), and *Limited* (*Ltd.*). In the names of academic presses, replace *University Press* with *UP* (or, if the words are separated by other words or appear alone, replace them with *U* and *P*: "U of Chicago P," "MIT P," "Teachers College P"). Otherwise, write publishers' names in full.

### 1.6.4 Titles of Works

A title in a parenthetical citation often has to be abbreviated. Usually the title is shortened to its initial noun phrase. Because the books of the Bible and works of Shakespeare are cited often, there are well-established abbreviations for their titles.

*see sec. 3.2.1*

#### *Bible*

The following abbreviations and spelled forms are commonly used for parts of the Bible (which may be abbreviated as *Bib.*). While the Hebrew Bible and the Protestant Old Testament include the same parts in slightly different arrangements, Roman Catholic versions of the Old Testament also include works listed here under "Selected Apocrypha."

**Hebrew Bible or Old Testament (OT)**

| | |
|---|---|
| Amos | Amos |
| Cant. of Cant. | Canticle of Canticles (also called Song of Solomon and Song of Songs) |
| 1 Chron. | 1 Chronicles |
| 2 Chron. | 2 Chronicles |
| Dan. | Daniel |
| Deut. | Deuteronomy |

| | |
|---|---|
| Eccles. | Ecclesiastes (also called Qoheleth) |
| Esth. | Esther |
| Exod. | Exodus |
| Ezek. | Ezekiel |
| Ezra | Ezra |
| Gen. | Genesis |
| Hab. | Habakkuk |
| Hag. | Haggai |
| Hos. | Hosea |
| Isa. | Isaiah |
| Jer. | Jeremiah |
| Job | Job |
| Joel | Joel |
| Jon. | Jonah |
| Josh. | Joshua |
| Judg. | Judges |
| 1 Kings | 1 Kings |
| 2 Kings | 2 Kings |
| Lam. | Lamentations |
| Lev. | Leviticus |
| Mal. | Malachi |
| Mic. | Micah |
| Nah. | Nahum |
| Neh. | Nehemiah |
| Num. | Numbers |
| Obad. | Obadiah |
| Prov. | Proverbs |
| Ps. | Psalms |
| Qoh. | Qoheleth (also called Ecclesiastes) |
| Ruth | Ruth |
| 1 Sam. | 1 Samuel |
| 2 Sam. | 2 Samuel |
| Song of Sg. | Song of Songs (also called Canticle of Canticles and Song of Solomon) |
| Song of Sol. | Song of Solomon (also called Canticle of Canticles and Song of Songs) |

| | |
|---|---|
| Zech. | Zechariah |
| Zeph. | Zephaniah |

**New Testament (NT)**

| | |
|---|---|
| Acts | Acts |
| Apoc. | Apocalypse (also called Revelation) |
| Col. | Colossians |
| 1 Cor. | 1 Corinthians |
| 2 Cor. | 2 Corinthians |
| Eph. | Ephesians |
| Gal. | Galatians |
| Heb. | Hebrews |
| Jas. | James |
| John | John |
| 1 John | 1 John |
| 2 John | 2 John |
| 3 John | 3 John |
| Jude | Jude |
| Luke | Luke |
| Mark | Mark |
| Matt. | Matthew |
| 1 Pet. | 1 Peter |
| 2 Pet. | 2 Peter |
| Phil. | Philippians |
| Philem. | Philemon |
| Rev. | Revelation (also called Apocalypse) |
| Rom. | Romans |
| 1 Thess. | 1 Thessalonians |
| 2 Thess. | 2 Thessalonians |
| 1 Tim. | 1 Timothy |
| 2 Tim. | 2 Timothy |
| Tit. | Titus |

**Selected Apocrypha**

| | |
|---|---|
| Bar. | Baruch |
| Bel and Dr. | Bel and the Dragon |

| | |
|---|---|
| Ecclus. | Ecclesiasticus (also called Sirach) |
| 1 Esd. | 1 Esdras |
| 2 Esd. | 2 Esdras |
| Esth. (Apocr.) | Esther (Apocrypha) |
| Jth. | Judith |
| 1 Macc. | 1 Maccabees |
| 2 Macc. | 2 Maccabees |
| Pr. of Man. | Prayer of Manasseh |
| Sg. of 3 Childr. | Song of Three Children |
| Sir. | Sirach (also called Ecclesiasticus) |
| Sus. | Susanna |
| Tob. | Tobit |
| Wisd. | Wisdom (also called Wisdom of Solomon) |
| Wisd. of Sol. | Wisdom of Solomon (also called Wisdom) |

**Works of Shakespeare**

| | |
|---|---|
| *Ado* | *Much Ado about Nothing* |
| *Ant.* | *Antony and Cleopatra* |
| *AWW* | *All's Well That Ends Well* |
| *AYL* | *As You Like It* |
| *Cor.* | *Coriolanus* |
| *Cym.* | *Cymbeline* |
| *Err.* | *The Comedy of Errors* |
| F1 | First Folio edition (1623) |
| F2 | Second Folio edition (1632) |
| *Ham.* | *Hamlet* |
| *1H4* | *Henry IV, Part 1* |
| *2H4* | *Henry IV, Part 2* |
| *H5* | *Henry V* |
| *1H6* | *Henry VI, Part 1* |
| *2H6* | *Henry VI, Part 2* |

| | |
|---|---|
| *3H6* | *Henry VI, Part 3* |
| *H8* | *Henry VIII* |
| *JC* | *Julius Caesar* |
| *Jn.* | *King John* |
| *LC* | *A Lover's Complaint* |
| *LLL* | *Love's Labour's Lost* |
| *Lr.* | *King Lear* |
| *Luc.* | *The Rape of Lucrece* |
| *Mac.* | *Macbeth* |
| *MM* | *Measure for Measure* |
| *MND* | *A Midsummer Night's Dream* |
| *MV* | *The Merchant of Venice* |
| *Oth.* | *Othello* |
| *Per.* | *Pericles* |
| *PhT* | *The Phoenix and the Turtle* |
| *PP* | *The Passionate Pilgrim* |
| Q | Quarto edition |
| *R2* | *Richard II* |
| *R3* | *Richard III* |
| *Rom.* | *Romeo and Juliet* |
| *Shr.* | *The Taming of the Shrew* |
| *Son.* | *Sonnets* |
| *TGV* | *The Two Gentlemen of Verona* |
| *Tim.* | *Timon of Athens* |
| *Tit.* | *Titus Andronicus* |
| *Tmp.* | *The Tempest* |
| *TN* | *Twelfth Night* |
| *TNK* | *The Two Noble Kinsmen* |
| *Tro.* | *Troilus and Cressida* |
| *Ven.* | *Venus and Adonis* |
| *Wiv.* | *The Merry Wives of Windsor* |
| *WT* | *The Winter's Tale* |

# 2 Works Cited

Following are details and special situations not covered in part 1.

## 2.1 Names of Authors

see pp. 21–22

The author's name should be presented last name first in the works-cited list and be copied from an authoritative location in your source. The guidelines below cover exceptions and complications that can crop up as you format authors' names.

### 2.1.1 Variant Forms

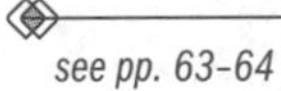

see pp. 63–64

The name of an author may be spelled in various ways in works you consult (e.g., Virgil, Vergil). Names from languages that do not use the Latin alphabet, like Chinese and Russian, may vary because of the systems of romanization used (e.g., Zhuang Zhou, Zhuangzi; Dostoyevsky, Dostoevsky). If an author's name varies, choose the variant preferred by your dictionary or another authority and list all the works by the author under that variant in your works-cited list.

A pseudonym that takes the traditional form of a first and last name should be given last name first in the works-cited list, like an author's real name. A pseudonym that does not take the traditional form should be given unchanged.

Film Crit Hulk
Tribble, Ivan

If you know the real name of an author listed under a pseudonym, you may add it in a parenthesis. Adding the real name is not essential for famous pseudonyms, like George Eliot, Stendhal, and Mark Twain, but may be useful for less familiar pseudonyms and is particularly desirable for online usernames.

Benton, Thomas H. (William Pannapacker)
@jmittell (Jason Mittell)

If your sources include works published under an author's real name and other works published under a pseudonym of the author, either consolidate the entries under the better-known name (e.g., Mark Twain rather than Samuel Clemens) or list them separately, with a cross-reference at the real name and with the real name in a parenthesis after the pseudonym.

Bakhtin, M. M. (*see also* Vološinov, V. N.). *The Dialogic Imagination: Four Essays.* Edited by Michael Holquist, translated by Caryl Emerson and Holquist, U of Texas P, 1981.

Vološinov, V. N. (M. M. Bakhtin). *Marxism and the Philosophy of Language.* Translated by Ladislav Matejka and I. R. Titunik, Harvard UP, 1986.

In the example for *The Dialogic Imagination: Four Essays*, one of the translators' names appears as a surname alone (Holquist), because his name has previously been given in full in the entry.

If works by the same person are published under different names, list each work under the appropriate name; you may include cross-references at both names.

Penelope, Julia (*see also* Stanley, Julia P.). "John Simon and the 'Dragons of Eden.'" *College English*, vol. 44, no. 8, Dec. 1982, pp. 848-54. *JSTOR*, www.jstor.org/stable/377341.

Stanley, Julia P. (*see also* Penelope, Julia). "'Correctness,' 'Appropriateness,' and the Uses of English." *College English*, vol. 41, no. 3, Nov. 1979, pp. 330-35. *JSTOR*, www.jstor.org/stable/376452.

## 2.1.2 Titles and Suffixes

In general, omit titles, affiliations, and degrees that precede or follow names.

| In Source Work | In Works-Cited List |
|---|---|
| Anthony T. Boyle, PhD | Boyle, Anthony T. |
| Sister Jean Daniel | Daniel, Jean |
| Sir Walter Scott | Scott, Walter |
| Saint Teresa de Jesús | Teresa de Jesús |

A suffix that is an essential part of the name—like *Jr.* or a roman numeral—appears after the given name, preceded by a comma.

Rockefeller, John D., IV
Rust, Arthur George, Jr.

### 2.1.3 Corporate Authors

Corporate authors in in-text citations *see sec. 3.1.2*

A work may be created by a corporate author—an institution, an association, a government agency, or another kind of organization. When a work's author and publisher are separate organizations, give both names, starting the entry with the one that is the author. When an organization is both author and publisher, begin the entry with the work's title, skipping the author element, and list the organization only as publisher. Do not include *The* before the name of any organization in the works-cited list.

When an entry starts with a government agency as the author, begin the entry with the name of the government, followed by a comma and the name of the agency. Between them, name any organizational units of which the agency is part (as, e.g., the House of Representatives is part of Congress). All the names are arranged from the largest entity to the smallest.

California, Department of Industrial Relations
United States, Congress, House

If you are documenting two or more works by the same government, substitute three hyphens for any name repeated from the author in the previous entry.

United States, Congress, House.
---, ---, Senate.
---, Department of Health and Human Services, Centers for Disease Control and Prevention.

Below are sample entries for government publications.

*The Adirondack Park in the Twenty-First Century*. Commission on the Adirondacks in the Twenty-First Century, New York State, 1990.

*Foreign Direct Investment, the Service Sector, and International Banking*. Centre on Transnational Corporations, United Nations, 1987.

Great Britain, Ministry of Agriculture, Fisheries, and Food. *Our Countryside, the Future: A Fair Deal for Rural England*. Her Majesty's Stationery Office, 2000.

New York State, Committee on State Prisons. *Investigation of the New York State Prisons*. 1883. Arno Press, 1974.

United Nations. *Consequences of Rapid Population Growth in Developing Countries*. Taylor and Francis, 1991.

At the end of entries for congressional publications, you may optionally include the number and session of Congress, the chamber (Senate or House of Representatives), and the type and number of the publication. Types of congressional publications include bills, resolutions, reports, and documents. If your project involves the use of many congressional publications, consult *The Chicago Manual of Style* for specialized guidelines on documenting them.

Poore, Benjamin Perley, compiler. *A Descriptive Catalogue of the Government Publications of the United States, September 5, 1774-March 4, 1881*. Government Printing Office, 1885. 48th Congress, 2nd session, Miscellaneous Document 67.

United States, Congress, House, Permanent Select Committee on Intelligence. *Al-Qaeda: The Many Faces of an Islamist Extremist Threat*. Government Printing Office, 2006. 109th Congress, 2nd session, House Report 615.

## 2.2 Titles

Titles should be stated in full in the works-cited list, including any subtitles. Regardless of where a title appears in your project—in the main text or in the works-cited list—its capitalization, punctuation, and presentation in italics or in quotation marks should be consistent.

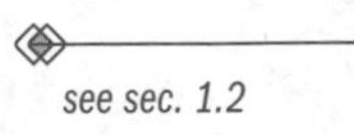
see sec. 1.2

## 2.2.1 Introduction, Preface, Foreword, or Afterword

To document an introduction, a preface, a foreword, or an afterword that is titled only with a descriptive term, capitalize the term in the works-cited list but neither italicize it nor enclose it in quotation marks.

> Felstiner, John. Preface. *Selected Poems and Prose of Paul Celan,* by Paul Celan, translated by Felstiner, W. W. Norton, 2001, pp. xix-xxxvi.

Last name only
see p. 103

The descriptive term remains capitalized if needed in an in-text citation but is lowercase if used in a text discussion.

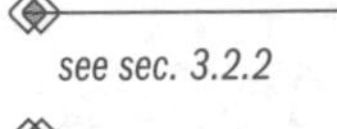
see sec. 3.2.2

see sec. 1.2.2

If the introduction, preface, foreword, or afterword has a unique title as well as a descriptive one, give the unique title, enclosed in quotation marks, immediately before the descriptive one.

> Wallach, Rick. "Cormac McCarthy's Canon as Accidental Artifact." Introduction. *Myth, Legend, Dust: Critical Responses to Cormac McCarthy,* edited by Wallach, Manchester UP, 2000, pp. xiv-xvi.

Then the unique title (or a short version of it) is given in an in-text citation if a title is needed.

## 2.2.2 Translations of Titles

In the works-cited list, translations of titles not in English, when needed for clarification, are placed in square brackets.

Šklovskij, Viktor. "Искусство, как прием" ["Art as Device"]. *О теории прозы* [*On the Theory of Prose*], 2nd reprint, 1929, Ardis Publishers, 1985, pp. 7-23.

## 2.3 Versions

Definition of a version *see pp. 38-39*

When citing versions in the works-cited list, write ordinal numbers with arabic numerals (*2nd*, *34th*) and abbreviate *revised* (*rev.*) and *edition* (*ed.*). Descriptive terms for versions, such as *expanded ed.* and *2nd ed.*, are written all lowercase, except that an initial letter directly following a period is capitalized.

*see sec. 1.6.2*

Cheyfitz, Eric. *The Poetics of Imperialism: Translation and Colonization from* The Tempest *to* Tarzan. Expanded ed., U of Pennsylvania P, 1997.

By contrast, names like Authorized King James Version and Norton Critical Edition are proper nouns (names of unique things) and are therefore capitalized like titles. Words in them are not abbreviated.

*see sec. 1.2.1*

*The Bible*. Authorized King James Version, Oxford UP, 1998.

Wollstonecraft, Mary. *A Vindication of the Rights of Woman*. Edited by Deidre Shauna Lynch, Norton Critical Edition, 3rd ed., W. W. Norton, 2009.

## 2.4 Publisher

The identity of a book's publisher may be unclear if more than one organization is named on the title page. The examples on pages 108–09 show how you can use evidence on the title page to determine the publisher.

# Determining the Publisher of a Book

## Copublishers

If more than one independent organization is identified in the source as the publisher, cite all the names, following the order shown in the source and separating the names with a forward slash. Below, for example, are two excerpts from title pages, followed by the publishers' names as recorded in the works-cited list.

> Published by The Pennsylvania State University Press
> for the Bibliographical Society of America
> University Park, Pennsylvania

Pennsylvania State UP / Bibliographical Society of America

> Iberoamericana · Vervuert · Librería Sur · 2013

Iberoamericana / Vervuert / Librería Sur

## Division

If the title page contains the names of a parent company and of a division of it, generally cite only the division. In the example at right, "Group" indicates that "Taylor and Francis" is the name of a combination of companies, of which Routledge is a part.

> LIVERIGHT PUBLISHING CORPORATION
> *A Division of W. W. Norton & Company*
> New York • London

ROUTLEDGE
Routledge
Taylor & Francis Group
LONDON AND NEW YORK

Liveright Publishing

Routledge

## Imprint

If the title page contains an imprint (a kind of brand name that the publisher attaches to some of its publications), as well as the publisher's name, omit the imprint. The wording and design on the title page may help you identify imprints. Given a title page with the information below, you would omit "An October Book"—an imprint.

AN OCTOBER BOOK

THE MIT PRESS
CAMBRIDGE, MASSACHUSETTS
LONDON, ENGLAND

MIT P

The wording and design of the excerpt below suggest that Vintage International is an imprint, named along with a division (Vintage Books) and a parent company (Random House). Only the name of the division should be cited.

*Vintage International*
**VINTAGE BOOKS**
**A DIVISION OF RANDOM HOUSE, INC.**
**NEW YORK**

Vintage Books

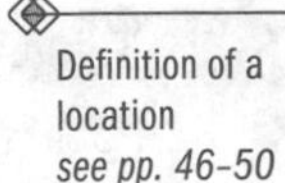
Definition of a location
*see pp. 46–50*

## 2.5 Locational Elements

### 2.5.1 Plus Sign with Page Number

If a work in a periodical (journal, magazine, newspaper) is not printed on consecutive pages, include only the first page number and a plus sign, leaving no intervening space.

> Williams, Joy. "Rogue Territory." *The New York Times Book Review*, 9 Nov. 2014, pp. 1+.

### 2.5.2 URLs and DOIs

When giving a URL, copy it in full from your Web browser, but omit *http://* or *https://*. Avoid citing URLs produced by shortening services (like bit.ly), since such a URL may stop working if the service that produced it disappears.

Articles in journals are often assigned DOIs, or digital object identifiers. A DOI will continue to lead to an object online even if the URL changes. DOIs consist of a series of digits (and sometimes letters), such as 10.1353/pmc.2000.0021. When possible, cite a DOI (preceded by *doi:*) instead of a URL.

> Chan, Evans. "Postmodernism and Hong Kong Cinema." *Postmodern Culture*, vol. 10, no. 3, May 2000. *Project Muse*, doi:10.1353/pmc.2000.0021.

## 2.6 Punctuation in the Works-Cited List

With a few exceptions, listed below, the punctuation in entries in the works-cited list is restricted to commas and periods. Periods are used after the author, after the title of the source, and at the end of the information for each container. Commas are used mainly with the author's name and between elements within each container.

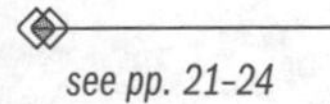
*see pp. 21–24*

### 2.6.1 Square Brackets

When a source does not indicate necessary facts about its publication, such as the name of the publisher or the date of publication, supply as much of the missing information as you can, enclosing it in square brackets to show that it did not come from the source. If a publication date that you supply is only approximated, put it after *circa* ("around").

[circa 2008]

If you are uncertain about the accuracy of the information that you supply, add a question mark.

[2008?]

If the city of publication is not included in the name of a locally published newspaper, add the city, not italicized, in square brackets after the name.

*The Star-Ledger* [Newark]

You need not add the city of publication to the name of a nationally published newspaper (e.g., *The Wall Street Journal*, *The Chronicle of Higher Education*).

### 2.6.2 Forward Slash

When a source presents multiple pieces of information for a single element in the entry—for instance, when more than one publisher is named—separate them with a forward slash.

see sec. 2.4

Tomlinson, Janis A., editor. *Goya: Images of Women*. National Gallery of Art / Yale UP, 2002.

## 2.7 Formatting and Ordering the Works-Cited List

The entries you create for your sources are gathered into a list, with the heading "Works Cited." (If the list contains only one entry, make the heading "Work Cited.") In

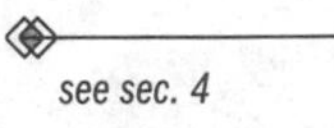
see sec. 4

a research paper, this list is usually placed at the end, after any endnotes. In other forms of academic work, the list may appear elsewhere.

Format the works-cited list so that the second and subsequent lines of each entry are indented half an inch from the left margin. This format, called *hanging indention*, helps the reader spot the beginning of each entry. When the creation of hanging indention is difficult—in certain digital contexts, for instance—leaving extra space between entries will serve the same purpose. The list is arranged in alphabetical order by the term that comes first in each entry: usually the author's last name but sometimes, when there is no author name, the title of the source.

### 2.7.1 Letter-by-Letter Alphabetization

The alphabetical ordering of entries that begin with authors' names is determined by the letters that come before the commas separating the authors' last and first names. Other punctuation marks and spaces are ignored. The letters following the commas are considered only when two or more last names are identical.

Descartes, René
De Sica, Vittorio

MacDonald, George
McCullers, Carson

Morris, Robert
Morris, William
Morrison, Toni

Saint-Exupéry, Antoine de
St. Denis, Ruth

Accents and other diacritical marks should be ignored in alphabetization: for example, *é* is treated the same as *e*. Special characters, such as @ in an online username, are also ignored.

## 2.7.2 Multiple Works by One Author

To document two or more works by the same author, give the author's name in the first entry only. Thereafter, in place of the name, type three hyphens. They stand for exactly the same name as in the preceding entry.

The three hyphens are usually followed by a period and then by the source's title. If the person named performed a role other than creating the work's main content, however, place a comma after the three hyphens and enter a term describing the role (*editor*, *translator*, *director*, etc.) before moving on to the title. If the same person performed such a role for two or more listed works, a suitable label for that role must appear in each entry. Multiple sources by the same person are alphabetized by their titles; terms describing the person's roles are not considered in alphabetization.

> Borroff, Marie. *Language and the Poet: Verbal Artistry in Frost, Stevens, and Moore.* U of Chicago P, 1979.
>
> ---, translator. Pearl*: A New Verse Translation.* W. W. Norton, 1977.
>
> ---. "Sound Symbolism as Drama in the Poetry of Robert Frost." *PMLA*, vol. 107, no. 1, Jan. 1992, pp. 131-44. *JSTOR*, www.jstor.org/stable/462806.
>
> ---, editor. *Wallace Stevens: A Collection of Critical Essays.* Prentice-Hall, 1963.

If a single author cited in one entry is also the first of multiple authors in the next entry, repeat the name in full; do not substitute three hyphens. Repeat the name in full whenever you cite the same person as part of a different team of authors.

> Tannen, Deborah. *Talking Voices: Repetition, Dialogue, and Imagery in Conversational Discourse.* 2nd ed., Cambridge UP, 2007. Studies in Interactional Sociolinguistics 26.

---. *You're Wearing That? Understanding Mothers and Daughters in Conversation.* Ballantine Books, 2006.

Tannen, Deborah, and Roy O. Freedle, editors. *Linguistics in Context: Connecting Observation and Understanding.* Ablex Publishing, 1988.

Tannen, Deborah, and Muriel Saville-Troike, editors. *Perspectives on Silence.* Ablex Publishing, 1985.

## 2.7.3 Multiple Works by Coauthors

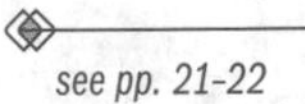
see pp. 21-22

If two or more entries citing coauthors begin with the same name, alphabetize them by the last names of the second authors listed.

Scholes, Robert, and Robert Kellogg
Scholes, Robert, and Eric S. Rabkin

To document two or more works by the same coauthors whose names appear in a consistent order in the works, give the names in the first entry only. Thereafter, in place of the names, type three hyphens, followed by a period and the title. The three hyphens stand for exactly the same names, in the same order, as in the preceding entry.

Gilbert, Sandra M., and Susan Gubar, editors. *The Female Imagination and the Modernist Aesthetic.* Gordon and Breach Science Publishers, 1986.

---. "Sexual Linguistics: Gender, Language, Sexuality." *New Literary History*, vol. 16, no. 3, Spring 1985, pp. 515-43. *JSTOR*, www.jstor.org/stable/468838.

If the coauthors' names do not appear in the same order in the source works, record the names as found in the works and alphabetize the entries accordingly.

### 2.7.4 Alphabetizing by Title

The alphabetization of an entry is based on the work's title in two situations. When no author is named at the start of the entry, the title determines the placement of the entry in the works-cited list. When the work's author appears at the start of more than one entry, the title determines the placement of the entry under the author's name.

see pp. 24-25

see sec. 2.7.2

Alphabetize titles letter by letter, ignoring any initial *A*, *An*, or *The* or the equivalent in other languages. For example, the title *An Encyclopedia of the Latin American Novel* would be alphabetized under *e* rather than *a* and the title *Le théâtre en France au Moyen Âge* under *t* rather than *l*.

see sec. 2.7.1

If the title begins with a numeral, alphabetize the title as if the numeral were spelled out. For instance, *1914: The Coming of the First World War* should be alphabetized as if it began with "Nineteen Fourteen."

### 2.7.5 Cross-References

To avoid unnecessary repetition in citing two or more sources from a collection of works such as an anthology, you may create a complete entry for the collection and cross-reference individual pieces to that entry. In a cross-reference, give the author and the title of the source; a reference to the full entry for the collection, usually consisting of the name or names starting the entry, followed by a short form of the collection's title, if needed; a comma; and the inclusive page or reference numbers.

> Agee, James. "Knoxville: Summer of 1915." Oates and Atwan, pp. 171-75.
>
> Angelou, Maya. "Pickin Em Up and Layin Em Down." Baker, *Norton Book*, pp. 276-78.
>
> Atwan, Robert. Foreword. Oates and Atwan, pp. x-xvi.
>
> Baker, Russell, editor. *The Norton Book of Light Verse*. W. W. Norton, 1986.

---, editor. *Russell Baker's Book of American Humor.* W. W. Norton, 1993.

Hurston, Zora Neale. "Squinch Owl Story." Baker, *Russell Baker's Book*, pp. 458-59.

Kingston, Maxine Hong. "No Name Woman." Oates and Atwan, pp. 383-94.

Lebowitz, Fran. "Manners." Baker, *Russell Baker's Book*, pp. 556-59.

Lennon, John. "The Fat Budgie." Baker, *Norton Book*, pp. 357-58.

Oates, Joyce Carol, and Robert Atwan, editors. *The Best American Essays of the Century.* Houghton Mifflin, 2000.

Rodriguez, Richard. "Aria: A Memoir of a Bilingual Childhood." Oates and Atwan, pp. 447-66.

Walker, Alice. "Looking for Zora." Oates and Atwan, pp. 395-411.

# 3 In-Text Citations

The goals of the in-text citation are brevity and clarity, guiding the reader as unobtrusively as possible to the corresponding entry in the works-cited list. Following are special situations not covered in part 1.

## 3.1 Author

### 3.1.1 Coauthors

see p. 21

If the entry in the works-cited list begins with the names of two authors, include both last names in the in-text citation, connected by *and*.

(Dorris and Erdrich 23)

see p. 22

If the source has three or more authors, the entry in the works-cited list begins with the first author's name followed by *et al.* The in-text citation follows suit.

(Burdick et al. 42)

### 3.1.2 Corporate Author

When a corporate author is named in a parenthetical citation, abbreviate terms that are commonly abbreviated, such as *Department* (*Dept.*). If the corporate author is identified in the works-cited list by the names of administrative units separated by commas, give all the names in the parenthetical citation.

see sec. 2.1.3

see sec. 1.6.2

In 1988 a federal report observed that the "current high level of attention to child care is directly attributable to the new workforce trends" (United States, Dept. of Labor 147).

Work Cited

United States, Department of Labor. *Child Care: A Workforce Issue.* Government Printing Office, 1988.

## 3.2 Title

### 3.2.1 Abbreviating Titles of Sources

When a title is needed in a parenthetical citation, abbreviate the title if it is longer than a noun phrase. For example, *Faulkner's Southern Novels* consists entirely of a noun phrase (a noun, *novels*, preceded by two modifiers) and would not be shortened. By contrast, *Faulkner's Novels of the South* can be shortened to its initial noun phrase, *Faulkner's Novels*. The abbreviated title should begin with the word by which the title is alphabetized. If possible, give the first noun and any preceding adjectives, while excluding any initial article: *a*, *an*, *the*.

**Full Titles**

*The Double Vision: Language and Meaning in Religion*

"Traveling in the Breakdown Lane: A Principle of Resistance for Hypertext"

"You Say You Want a Revolution? Hypertext and the Laws of Media"

**Abbreviations**

*Double Vision*
"Traveling"
"You"

If the title does not begin with a noun phrase, cite the first word if it is enough to direct the reader to the correct entry.

**Full Titles**

*And Quiet Flows the Don*
*Can We Say No? The Challenge of Rationing Health Care*
*Under the Volcano*

**Abbreviations**

*And*
*Can*
*Under*

In some kinds of studies, it is necessary to cite the books of the Bible or the works of Shakespeare frequently—for instance, studies tracing a theme in the Bible or in Shakespeare's plays. There are well-established abbreviations for the titles of these works, which you may use to make your citations concise. First, create an entry in the works-cited list for the edition of the Bible or of Shakespeare's works that you used. Then, when you borrow from the edition, use the relevant title abbreviation, along with the part numbers, in the parenthetical citation (unless you've mentioned the title in your text): for example, "1 Chron. 21.8" or "Rev. 21.3," for the Bible, and "*Oth.* 4.2.7–13" or "*Mac.* 1.5.17," for Shakespeare.

see sec. 1.6.4

see sec. 3.3.2

## 3.2.2 Descriptive Terms in Place of Titles

If a work is identified in the works-cited list by a descriptive term, not by a unique title, cite the term or a shortened version of it in place of the title if a title needs to be included in a parenthetical citation. The descriptive term should be

see pp. 28–29, sec. 2.2.1

see sec. 3.2.1

capitalized exactly as in the works-cited list and be neither italicized nor enclosed in quotation marks.

Margaret Drabble describes how publishers sometimes pressured Lessing to cut controversial details from her work—or to add them (Introduction xi-xii).

Americans' "passion for material objects" reached a "climactic moment in the 1880s and 1890s" (Werner, Review 622).

Works Cited

Drabble, Margaret. Introduction. *Stories*, by Doris Lessing, Alfred A. Knopf, 2008, pp. vii-xvii. Everyman's Library 316.

---. *The Millstone*. Harcourt Brace, 1998.

Werner, Marta L. "Helen Keller and Anne Sullivan: Writing Otherwise." *Textual Cultures*, vol. 5, no. 1, Spring 2010, pp. 1-45.

---. Review of *A Sense of Things: The Object Matter of American Literature* and *Surface and Depth: The Quest for Legibility in American Culture*. *American Literature*, vol. 76, no. 3, Sept. 2004, pp. 622-24.

## 3.3 Numbers in In-Text Citations

### 3.3.1 Style of Numerals

When you cite pages in a print work, use the same style of numerals as in the source—whether roman (traditionally used in the front matter of books), arabic, or a specialized style, like *A1* (sometimes found in newspapers). Use arabic numerals in all your other references to divisions of works (volumes, sections, books, chapters, acts, scenes, etc.), even if the numbers appear otherwise in the source.

If you borrow from only one volume of a multivolume work, the number of the volume is specified in the entry in the works-cited list and does not need to be included in

see p. 39

the in-text citations. If you borrow from more than one volume, include a volume number as well as a page reference in the in-text citations, separating the two with a colon and a space. Use neither the words *volume* and *page* nor their abbreviations. The functions of the numbers in such a citation are understood.

> As Wellek admits in the middle of his multivolume history of modern literary criticism, "An evolutionary history of criticism must fail. I have come to this resigned conclusion" (5: xxii).
>
> Work Cited
>
> Wellek, René. *A History of Modern Criticism, 1750-1950*. Yale UP, 1955-92. 8 vols.

Total number of volumes
*see pp. 51-52*

If you refer parenthetically to an entire volume of a multivolume work, place a comma after the author's name and include the abbreviation *vol.*

> Between 1945 and 1972, the political-party system in the United States underwent profound changes (Schlesinger, vol. 4).
>
> Work Cited
>
> Schlesinger, Arthur M., Jr., general editor. *History of U.S. Political Parties*. Chelsea House Publishers, 1973. 4 vols.

If you integrate such a reference into a sentence, spell out *volume*: "In volume 2, Wellek deals with. . . ."

## 3.3.2 Numbers in Works Available in Multiple Editions

Commonly studied literary works are frequently available in more than one edition. In citations of a work available in multiple editions, it is often helpful to provide division numbers in addition to, or instead of, page numbers, so that readers can find your references in any edition of the work.

### *Modern Prose Works*

In a reference to a commonly studied modern prose work, such as a novel or a play in prose, give the page number first, add a semicolon, and then give other identifying information, using appropriate abbreviations: "(130; ch. 9)," "(271; book 4, ch. 2)."

see sec. 1.6.2

> In *A Vindication of the Rights of Woman,* Mary Wollstonecraft recollects many "women who, not led by degrees to proper studies, and not permitted to choose for themselves, have indeed been overgrown children" (185; ch. 13, sec. 2).
>
> Willy Loman admits to his wife, "I have such thoughts, I have such strange thoughts" (Miller 9; act 1).

### *Modern Verse Works*

Editions of commonly studied poems and verse plays sometimes provide line numbers in the margins. In citing works in verse with line numbering, omit page numbers altogether and cite by division (act, scene, canto, book, part) and line, separating the numbers with periods—for example, "*Iliad* 9.19" refers to book 9, line 19, of Homer's *Iliad.* If you are citing only line numbers, do not use the abbreviation *l.* or *ll.*, which can be confused with numerals. Instead, in your first citation, use the word *line* or *lines* and then, having established that the numbers designate lines, give the numbers alone.

> According to the narrator of Felicia Hemans's poem, the emerging prisoners "had learn'd, in cells of secret gloom, / How sunshine is forgotten!" (lines 131-32).
>
> One Shakespearean protagonist seems resolute at first when he asserts, "Haste me to know't, that I, with wings as swift / As meditation . . . / May sweep to my revenge" (*Ham.* 1.5.35-37), but he soon has second thoughts; another tragic figure, initially described as "too full o' th' milk of human kindness" (*Mac.* 1.5.17), quickly descends into horrific slaughter.

Do not count lines manually if no line numbers are present in the source; doing so would obligate your reader to do the same. Instead, cite page numbers or another explicit division numbering, if available (e.g., "canto 12"). If the work is a poem that occupies a page or less in the source edition, there is no need to cite line numbers or any other numbers in your text. (The poem's page number will appear in the works-cited list if the source is printed.)

If the work contains a mixture of prose and verse, determine which form of writing is predominant and use the corresponding citation format. For example, Shakespeare's plays are usually treated as works in verse, although they contain prose passages.

### *Greek, Roman, and Medieval Works*

Works in prose and verse from ancient Greece and Rome, as well as some medieval texts, are generally not cited by page number alone. The text's division numbers are given. The divisions cited may differ from one work to another. For example, Aristotle's works are commonly cited by the page, column, and line in a landmark 1831 edition of the Greek text. Thus, "1453a15–16" means lines 15–16 of the left-hand column ("a") on page 1453 of the 1831 edition. These indicators appear in the margins of modern editions of Aristotle's works.

### *Scripture*

see sec. 1.2.2

When documenting scripture, provide an entry in the works-cited list for the edition you consulted. While general terms like Bible, Talmud, and Koran are not italicized, full and shortened titles of specific editions are italicized. The first time you borrow from a particular work of scripture in your project, state in the text or in a parenthetical citation the element that begins the entry in the works-cited list (usually the title of the edition but sometimes an editor's or a translator's name). Identify the borrowing by divisions of the work—for the Bible, give the abbreviated name of the book and chapter and verse numbers—rather than by a page number. Subsequent citations of the same edition may provide division numbers alone.

see sec. 3.2.1

> In one of the most vivid prophetic visions in the Bible, Ezekiel saw "what seemed to be four living creatures," each with the faces of a man, a lion, an ox, and an eagle (*New Jerusalem Bible*, Ezek. 1.5-10). John of Patmos echoes this passage when describing his vision (Rev. 4.6-8).
>
> Work Cited
>
> *The New Jerusalem Bible.* General editor, Henry Wansbrough, Doubleday, 1985.

### 3.3.3 Other Citations Not Involving Page Numbers

Other kinds of sources may employ location indicators besides page numbers. An e-book (a work formatted for reading on an electronic device) may include a numbering system that tells users their location in the work. Because such numbering may vary from one device to another, do not cite it unless you know that it appears consistently to other users. If the work is divided into stable numbered sections like chapters, the numbers of those sections may be cited, with a label identifying the type of part that is numbered.

> According to Hazel Rowley, Franklin and Eleanor Roosevelt began their honeymoon with a week's stay at Hyde Park (ch. 2).

Part numbers in any source should be cited only if they are explicit (visible in the document) and fixed (the same for all users of the document). Do not count unnumbered parts manually. A source without page numbers or any other form of explicit, fixed part numbering must be cited as a whole:

include in the text or in a parenthesis enough information for the reader to find the corresponding entry in the works-cited list—usually the author's last name.

## 3.4 Indirect Sources

Whenever you can, take material from the original source, not a secondhand one. Sometimes, however, only an indirect source is available—for example, an author's published account of someone's spoken remarks. If what you quote or paraphrase is itself a quotation, put the abbreviation *qtd. in* ("quoted in") before the indirect source you cite in your parenthetical reference. (You may wish to clarify the relation between the original and secondhand sources in a note.)

> Samuel Johnson admitted that Edmund Burke was an "extraordinary man" (qtd. in Boswell 2: 450).

## 3.5 Repeated Use of Sources

When you borrow from a source several times in succession, you may be able to make your citations more concise by using one of the following techniques. Always give your citations in full, however, if these techniques would create ambiguity about your sources.

If you borrow more than once from the same source within a single paragraph and no other source intervenes, you may give a single parenthetical reference after the last borrowing.

> *Romeo and Juliet* presents an opposition between two worlds: "the world of the everyday . . . and the world of romance." Although the two lovers are part of the world of romance, their language of love nevertheless becomes "fully responsive to the tang of actuality" (Zender 138, 141).

This structure makes clear that the first page number in the parenthesis applies to the first quotation and the second number to the second quotation.

But suppose you decide to break the first quotation into two parts, instead of using an ellipsis. Then the parenthetical citation will be ambiguous, because three quotations will be followed by two numbers. It will not be clear how the page numbers should be matched to the borrowings. In that case, the citations should be separated. You can use another technique for making citations more economical—not repeating what is understood.

> *Romeo and Juliet* presents an opposition between two worlds: "the world of the everyday," associated with the adults in the play, and "the world of romance," associated with the two lovers (Zender 138). Romeo and Juliet's language of love nevertheless becomes "fully responsive to the tang of actuality" (141).

The second parenthetical citation, "(141)," omits the author's name. This omission is acceptable because the reader can only conclude that the author is Zender. If you include material from a different source between the two borrowings, however, you must repeat this author's name in the second citation: "(Zender 141)."

A third technique is to define a source in the text at the start.

> According to Karl F. Zender, *Romeo and Juliet* presents an opposition between two worlds: "the world of the everyday," associated with the adults in the play, and "the world of romance," associated with the two lovers (138). Romeo and Juliet's language of love nevertheless becomes "fully responsive to the tang of actuality" (141).

This technique can be useful when an entire paragraph is based on material from a single source. When a source is stated in this way and followed by a sequence of borrowings, it is important to signal at the end of the borrowings that you are switching to another source or to your own ideas.

> According to Karl F. Zender, *Romeo and Juliet* presents an opposition between two worlds: "the world of the everyday," associated with the adults in the play, and "the world of romance," associated with the two lovers (138). Romeo and Juliet's language of love nevertheless becomes "fully responsive to the tang of actuality" (141). I believe, in addition, that . . .

## 3.6 Punctuation in the In-Text Citation

No punctuation is used in a basic parenthetical citation, consisting of a number or of an author's last name and a number. When parenthetical citations are more complex, they must be punctuated for clarity.

Citations of multiple sources in a single parenthesis are separated by semicolons.

> (Baron 194; Jacobs 55)

Citations of different locations in a single source are separated by commas.

> (Baron 194, 200, 197-98)

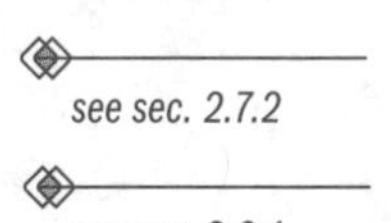

see sec. 2.7.2
see sec. 3.2.1

In a citation of multiple works by the same author, the titles (shortened if necessary) are joined by *and* if there are two; otherwise, they are listed with commas and *and*.

> (Glück, "Ersatz Thought" and "For")
> (Glück, "Ersatz Thought," "For," and Foreword)

Your explanation of how you altered a quotation is separated from the citation by a semicolon.

see sec. 1.3.6
see sec. 1.3.5
see p. 56

> (Baron 194; my emphasis)
> (29; 1st ellipsis in original)

If the number in a citation is not a page number or line number, it is usually preceded by a label identifying the type of part that is numbered. A comma separates such a reference from the author's name.

(Chan, par. 41)
(Rowley, ch. 2)

In a citation of commonly studied literature, a semicolon separates a page number from other part references. The other part references are separated by a comma.

see sec. 3.3.2

(185; ch. 13, sec. 2)

When a quotation from a non-English work is given bilingually, a parenthesis may begin with the translation or the original version and continue with the sources of the two versions. All these elements are separated by semicolons.

see sec. 1.3.8

At the opening of Dante's *Inferno*, the poet finds himself in "una selva oscura" ("a dark wood"; 1.2; Ciardi 28).

If a parenthetical citation falls in the same place in your text as another kind of parenthesis, do not put the two parentheses side by side. Instead, enclose both pieces of information in a single parenthesis, placing the more immediately relevant one first and enclosing the other in square brackets.

In *The American Presidency*, Sidney M. Milkis and Michael Nelson describe how "the great promise of the personal presidency was widely celebrated" during Kennedy's time in office—a mere thousand days (20 January 1961-22 November 1963 [325]).

# 4 Citations in Forms Other Than Print

Throughout its history, the *MLA Handbook* has focused on the production of scholarship in traditional, printed form. Before the eighth edition, the title declared that the handbook was for "writers of research papers," and the contents gave advice on structuring and formatting such papers. Today academic work can take many forms other than the research paper. Scholars produce presentations, videos, and interactive Web projects, among other kinds of work. Where these projects rely on the work of other authors, however, they should still include information about their sources.

How to include such information in projects other than the research paper is not yet a settled matter, but we offer a few suggestions. The standards for source documentation in nonprint forms are certain to change as media themselves change, but the aims will remain the same: providing the information that enables a curious reader, viewer, or other user to track down your sources and giving credit to those whose work influenced yours.

In a slide-based presentation using software such as *PowerPoint* or *Keynote*, we suggest including brief citations on each slide that uses borrowed material (quotations, paraphrases, images, videos, and whatever else you copy or adapt) and adding a works-cited list on a slide at the end. You might also offer printed copies of your works-cited list to your audience, if the venue of the presentation allows for them, or post the list online and include its URL on your works-cited slide.

In a video, you might overlay text at the bottom of the screen to provide your viewers with brief information about what they're seeing (the producer and title of a borrowed video clip, for instance, or the name of a person being interviewed) and include full documentation in your closing credits.

In a project on the Web, you might link from your citations to the online materials you cite, allowing a reader to follow references of interest. A works-cited list remains desirable as an appendix to the project, since it gives the reader an organized account of the full range of your sources.

# Practice Template

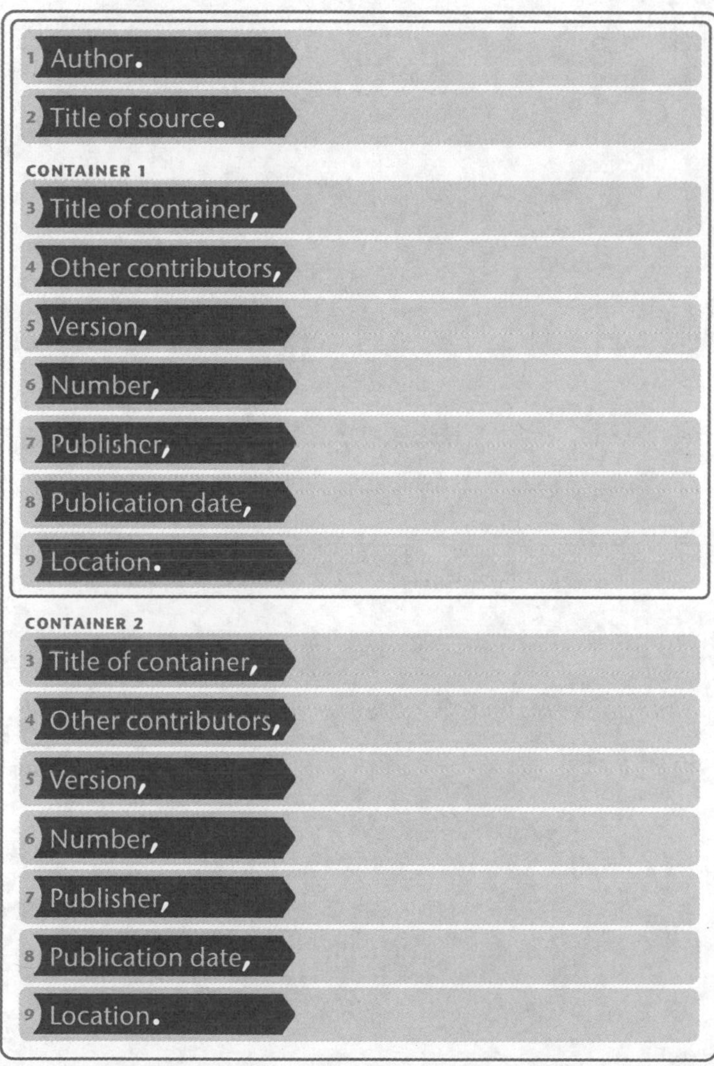

1 Author.
2 Title of source.
CONTAINER 1
3 Title of container,
4 Other contributors,
5 Version,
6 Number,
7 Publisher,
8 Publication date,
9 Location.
CONTAINER 2
3 Title of container,
4 Other contributors,
5 Version,
6 Number,
7 Publisher,
8 Publication date,
9 Location.


From *MLA Handbook* (8th ed.), published by the Modern Language Association (style.mla.org).

# Index

Numbers in italics (e.g., *1.4.1*) denote sections in part 2. The other numbers are page numbers in both parts of the handbook.


@, in online usernames 24
  ignored in alphabetization *2.7.1*
*a, an* *See* articles (*a, an, the*)
abbreviations *1.6*
  of common academic terms *1.6.2*
  in in-text citations
    authors' first names 55
    corporate authors *3.1.2*
    indirect sources (*qtd. in*) *3.4*
    three or more authors (*et al.*) *3.1.1*
    titles of sources 55–56, *1.6.4*, *3.2.1*
  in text
    numbers with abbreviations *1.4.1*
    titles of sources *1.2.3*
    use of periods *1.6*
  in works-cited lists
    editions 2.3
    months *1.5*, *1.6.1*
    publishers' names *1.6.2–3*
    versions *2.3*
academic disciplines, documentation styles in 5–6
academic integrity 6 *See also* plagiarism
academic presses, names of *1.6.3*
academic writing
  as conversation x, xii–xiii, 5
  cyclic nature of 12
  diversity of 127–28
  evaluating sources for 4, 10–12
  *See also* documentation; plagiarism; prose style and mechanics
accents, ignored in alphabetization *2.7.1*
access dates, for online sources 53
accuracy of quotations *1.3.1*
actors, in works-cited lists 24
addresses, spoken *See* live presentations
addresses, street *1.4.2*
adjectives
  capitalized in titles *1.2.1*
  in languages other than English *1.2.5*
  in shortened titles *3.2.1*
adverbs
  capitalized in titles *1.2.1*
  in languages other than English *1.2.5*
  in shortened titles *3.2.1*

afterwords
  documenting *2.2.1*
  referred to in text 70
*ALA-LC Romanization Tables* 64, 74
albums *See* recordings, audio
alphabetization
  of names not in English *1.1.4*
    Asian languages 63–64
    French 64
    German 64–65
    Italian 65
    Latin 65–66
    Spanish 66
  in works-cited lists *2.7.1–4*
    authors' names 21, 22, *2.7.2–3*
    letter by letter *2.7.1*
    no author *2.7.4*
    titles *2.7.4*
*and*
  between authors' names 21
  between editors' names 23
anonymous works 24, 55–56, *2.7.4*
anthologies *See* book collections
appendixes
  referred to in text 70
  works-cited lists as, in Web projects 128
Arabic, quotations and titles of sources in 74, *1.3.8*
arabic numerals *See* numbers; page numbers
archives
  locations of objects in 49–50
  online 11, 41–43, 45, 48
Aristotle, works of 122
articles (*a*, *an*, *the*)
  excluded in in-text citations *3.2.1*
  ignored in alphabetization *2.7.4*
  not capitalized in titles *1.2.1*
  omitted in corporate author names *2.1.3*
articles, online and print
  quotation marks around titles of *1.2.2*
  in works-cited lists
    author's names 21, 24, *2.1.1*
    digital platforms 31, 32
    page numbers, consecutive 46
    page numbers, not consecutive *2.5.1*
    pseudonyms 24, *2.1.1*
    publication dates 42–43, 44–45
    republication in book collections 53
    titles 27–28, 30
    URLs and DOIs 17, 48, 49, 128, *2.5.2*
  *See also* book collections; book reviews, in works-cited lists; periodicals; Web sites
artworks, in works-cited lists
  generic descriptions of 28–29
  locations of 49–50
Asian languages
  names of persons in 62, 63–64, *2.1.1*
  quotations and titles of sources in 74, *1.3.8*
audio recordings *See* film, television, and video; recordings, audio
authority of sources 4, 10–12
authors
  definition of 22–25
  evaluating reliability of 11
  *See also* authors' names; corporate authors
authors' names
  gathering information on 13, 14–17, *2.1*
  in in-text citations 54–58
    authors with same last names 55
    coauthors *3.1.1*

authors' names, in in-text citations *(cont.)*
multiple works by one author 55, *3.6*
single authors 54–55
in text
first and subsequent uses of names *1.1.1*
names not in English *1.1.4*
pseudonyms and simplified names *1.1.3*
titles of persons *1.1.2*
in works-cited lists
absence of author 24, 55–56
alphabetization *See* alphabetization
coauthors 21–23, *2.7.3*
cross-references *2.1.1*, *2.7.5*
film and television personnel 24
married names *2.1.1*
multiple works by one author *2.1.3*, *2.7.2*
pseudonyms and online usernames 24, *2.1.1*
punctuation 20, 21–22
titles and suffixes 72–74, *1.1.2*, *2.1.2*
translators 23
variant forms of names *2.1.1*
*See also* corporate authors; editors, in works-cited lists; names of persons; other contributors; translators' names

Bible
abbreviations for *1.6.4*
Apocrypha 99–100
New Testament 99
Old Testament and Hebrew Bible 97–99
in in-text citations 122–23, *1.6.4*, *3.2.1*
Bible *(cont.)*
in text, treatment of titles of 69
in works-cited lists 38, 123, *2.3*
bibliographies, referred to in text 70
blogs
as parts of networks of blogs 31
republication of posts 3
in works-cited lists
comments 29, 44
publishers 41–42
titles 28, 30
URLs 48, 49
*See also* articles, online and print
book collections
digital platforms for 31, 34
gathering information on 16
in works-cited lists
cross-references *2.7.5*
other contributors 38
page numbers 46
prior publication 50, 53
publication dates for articles 42
titles and subtitles 26–27, 30, 35
*See also* articles, online and print; editors, in works-cited lists; multivolume works
book reviews, untitled 29 *See also* articles, online and print
books
electronic *See* e-books
in text
capitalization and punctuation of titles *1.2.1*
italics for titles *1.2.2*
referring to parts of books 70
shortened titles *1.2.3*

books, in text *(cont.)*
titles not in English *1.2.5*
titles within titles *1.2.4*
in works-cited lists
author's names 21–25, *2.1*, *2.7.2–3*
editions 38–39
other contributors 37–38
prior publication 50, 53
publication dates 15, 45, 46
titles and subtitles 25–27, *2.2*
*See also* book collections; comic books; multivolume works; title pages; titles of containers; titles of sources
book series
titles of 69
in works-cited lists 52
*See also* multivolume works
brackets *See* square brackets

calendars *See* dates and times; years
capitalization
in text
parts of works 70
titles of sources in English *1.2.1*
titles of sources not in English *1.2.5*
in works-cited lists
editions 2.3
generic descriptions of sources 29
introductions, prefaces, forewords, and afterwords *2.2.1*
titles of sources 25–26, *1.2.1*
untitled sources 29
versions 38–39, *2.3*
CDs *See* recordings, audio
centuries *1.5* *See also* dates and times
chapter numbers *See* part numbers, other than page numbers
chapters, referred to in text 70 *See also* part numbers, other than page numbers
characters, fictional *1.1.3*
*Chicago Manual of Style, The* 64, 74, 105
Chinese
names of persons in 62, 63–64, *2.1.1*
quotations and titles of sources in 74, *1.3.8*
*circa* *2.6.1*
citations *See* in-text citations
cities of publication
of books 51
of newspapers *2.6.1*
coauthors
in in-text citations *3.1.1*
in works-cited lists 21–23, *2.7.3*
colons
before block quotations 87, *1.3.2–3*
with quotation marks 89
in titles *1.2.1*
comic books
titles of 31
volume and issue numbers of 40
commas
in in-text citations *3.6*
in numbers *1.4.2*
with quotation marks 88–89
in works-cited lists 20, *2.6*
authors' names 21, 22
other contributors 37
comments, online 29, 44
common knowledge, documentation unneeded for 10
compilers, in works-cited lists *2.1.3*
conference titles 70
conjunctions, in titles *1.2.1* *See also and*

containers *See* titles of containers
copublishers *2.4*
copyright pages
  publication dates on 15, 45, 46
  publishers' names on 41
corporate authors
  in in-text citations 55–56, *3.1.2*
  in works-cited lists 25, *2.1.3*
course titles 70
cross-references, in works-cited lists
  for varying names of authors *2.1.1*
  for works in collections *2.7.5*

*da*, *de*, *del*, etc., in Italian last names 65
databases *See* online databases
dates and times *1.5*
  abbreviations for *1.6*
  of access, for online works 53
*de*, *del*, and *y*, in Spanish last names 66
*de*, *du*, and *des*, in French last names 64
descriptive terms
  for documenting introductions, prefaces, forewords, and afterwords *2.2.1*
  for editors 23
  for film and television personnel 24
  for other contributors 37–38
  for parts of works in text 70
  in place of titles in citations *3.2.2*
  for unexpected types of works 52
  for untitled sources 28–29
diacritics, ignored in alphabetization *2.7.1*
dialogue
  quotations consisting solely of *1.3.7*
  quoted from plays or screenplays *1.3.4*
digital media
  dates needed for 42–43, 44–45
  gathering information on 17
  in works-cited lists
    publishers 41–42
    titles of containers 31–35
    URLs and DOIs 17, 48, 49, 128, *2.5.2*
    versions 39
  *See also* articles, online and print; blogs; Web sites
digital object identifiers (DOIs) 48, *2.5.2*
digital reference managers 12
directors, film and television *See* film, television, and video
*Doctor*, *Dr.*, use of title *1.1.2*
documentation
  commonsense approach to xii–xiii, 3–4
  development of MLA style of x–xii
  evaluating sources for 3, 10–12
  gathering information for 13–18
  importance of 5–6
  in-text citations and 54–58
  organizing information for 19
  recordkeeping and 8, 9–10, 12
  in research projects in nonprint media 127–28
  *See also* in-text citations; sources; works-cited lists
DOIs (digital object identifiers) 48, *2.5.2*
drama and plays
  quotations of *1.3.4*
  titles of 27, *1.2.2*
  *See also* book collections

DVDs
  disc numbers in sets of 49
  release dates of 44
  *See also* film, television, and video

e-books
  digital platforms for 31, 34, 47
  location indicators in *3.3.3*
  *See also* digital media
*ed.* *2.3*
editions
  publication dates of 45, 46
  works in multiple 57, *3.3.2*
editors, in works-cited lists
  multiple works by *2.7.2*
  multivolume works and 36
  as other contributors 37–38
  at start of entry 23
  three or more 23, 38
  two 23
  *See also* authors' names; book collections; other contributors
*e.g.* *1.6.2*
electronic books *See* e-books
ellipses, in quotations *1.3.5*
e-mail messages, in works-cited lists 29
*emphasis added*, use of *1.3.6*
essays
  in containers 32
  titles of 27–28, *1.2.2*
  *See also* book collections
*et al.* *1.6.2*
  in in-text citations *3.1.1*
  in works-cited lists 22, 23, 38
ethics and documentation 6 *See also* plagiarism
exclamation points and quotations 1.3.7
extracts *See* quotations

fictional characters *1.1.3*
film, television, and video
  digital platforms for 31, 33
  gathering information on 18
  research projects as 128
  timings in 57
  in works-cited lists
    contributors treated as authors 24
    disc numbers in DVD sets 49
    networks of airing 43
    other contributors 38
    production or distribution companies 41
    release dates 43–44
    seasons and episode numbers 40
    series and episode titles 24, 28, 30, 33
    URLs 48, 49
    versions 39
  *See also* dialogue
first lines of poems, as titles *1.2.1*
forewords
  documenting *2.2.1*
  referred to in text 70
forums, online, in works-cited lists 29, 44
forward slashes
  for line and stanza breaks in poetry *1.3.3*
  in works-cited lists
    separating comparable items *2.6.2*
    separating copublishers *2.4*
fraud *See* plagiarism
French
  names of persons in 64
  titles of sources in 72
front matter, of books
  documenting *2.2.1*
  referred to in text 70

German
names of persons in 64–65
titles of sources in 72–73
*Google* 12
governments and government agencies *See* corporate authors
Greek
documenting ancient works in 122
quotations and titles of sources in 74, *1.3.8*

hanging indention
for quoted dialogue *1.3.4*
for quoted poetry 79
in works-cited lists *2.7*
Hebrew, quotations and titles of sources in 74, *1.3.8*
Hungarian, names of persons in 62
hyphens
for authors' names in works-cited lists *2.1.3*, *2.7.2–3*
and capitalization, in compound terms *1.2.1*
in person's names *1.1.1*

*i.e.* *1.6.2*
imprints, publishers' 109
indention
of quotations 55, 76–77
of quotations with translations *1.3.8*
of quoted dialogue *1.3.4*
unusual, in quoted poetry 79
*See also* hanging indention; quotations
infinitives, not capitalized in titles *1.2.1*
institutions
objects in 49–50
romanizing non-English names of *1.3.8*
*See also* corporate authors

Internet
finding and retrieving sources on 11
research papers purchased on 7–8
URLs and DOIs and 17, 48, 49, 128, *2.5.2*
*See also* articles, online and print; digital media; online databases; online usernames, of authors; search engines; Web sites
in-text citations 54–58, *3.1–6*
abbreviations in
authors' first names 55
corporate authors *3.1.2*
indirect sources (*qtd. in*) *3.4*
three or more authors (*et al.*) *3.1.1*
titles of sources 55–56, *1.6.4*, *3.2.1*
coauthors in *3.1.1*
corporate authors in 55–56, *3.1.2*
descriptive terms in *3.2.2*
goals of 19, 54, 58, 116
indirect sources in *3.4*
introductions, prefaces, forewords, and afterwords in *2.2.1*
multiple sources in *3.6*
multivolume works in *3.3.1*
numbers in
location indicators other than pages *3.3.2–3*, *3.6*
style *3.3.1*
works in multiple editions *3.3.2*
organizing information for 19
punctuation and formatting of 54–58, 82, *1.3.2*, *1.3.7*, *3.6*
repeated use of sources and *3.5*

in-text citations *(cont.)*
shortened titles of legal cases in *1.2.3*
translations of quotations and *1.3.8*
*See also* quotations; works-cited lists
introductions
documenting *2.2.1*
referred to in text 70
Italian
names of persons in 65
titles of sources in 73
italics
in text
added to quotations *1.3.6*
titles of sources *1.2.2*
titles within titles *1.2.4*
in works-cited lists
titles of containers 30, 31
titles of sources 25–29, *1.2.2*

Japanese
names of persons in 62, 63
quotations and titles of sources in 74, *1.3.8*
journals *See* periodicals

*Keynote*, research projects presented with 128
Koran (Quran, Qur'an) 69, 122–23
Korean, names of persons in 62, 63

language *See* prose style and mechanics
languages other than English
capitalization in *1.2.5*
French 72
German 72–73
Italian 73
Latin 73–74
Spanish 74
languages other than English *(cont.)*
names of persons in *1.1.4*
Asian languages 62, 63–64
first and subsequent uses in text *1.1.1*
French 64
German 64–65
Italian 65
Latin 65–66
Spanish 66
variant forms of names *2.1.1*
titles of sources in *1.2.5*
French 72
German 72–73
initial articles ignored in alphabetizing *2.7.4*
Italian 73
Latin 73–74
other languages 75
romanized languages 74
Spanish 74
translations *1.2.5*, *2.2.2*
*See also* translations; translators' names
Latin
documenting ancient works in 122
names of persons in 65–66
titles of sources in 73–74
laws, titles of 69 *See also* legislative bills, reports, and resolutions
lectures *See* live presentations
legal cases, shortened titles of *1.2.3*
legislative bills, reports, and resolutions
titles of, in text 69
in works-cited lists 53, *2.1.3*
lists of works cited *See* works-cited lists
literary works, commonly studied
fictional characters in *1.1.3*

literary works, commonly studied *(cont.)*
in in-text citations
format and punctuation *1.3.2, 1.3.7, 3.6*
numbers 57, *3.3.2*
*See also* Bible; Shakespeare, William, works of; versions
live presentations
research projects as 128
in works-cited lists
descriptive terms 52
other contributors 38
venue, city, and date 50
*See also* recordings, audio
locations 46, 48–50, *2.5*
gathering information on 14
in works-cited lists
disc numbers in DVD sets 49
objects located in places 49–50
page numbers 46
page numbers not consecutive in periodicals *2.5.1*
URLs and DOIs 17, 48, 49, 128, *2.5.2*

magazines *See* periodicals
manuscripts
dates of *1.5*
locations of 50
married names, of authors *2.1.1*
measurements, writing of *1.4.1*
mechanics, prose *See* prose style and mechanics
medieval works, documenting 122
messages, online, in works-cited lists 29
*MLA Handbook*, history of x–xii
months, abbreviations for *1.5, 1.6.1* *See also* dates and times
multiple authors
in in-text citations *3.1.1*
in works-cited lists 21–23, *2.7.3*
multivolume works
in in-text citations *3.3.1*
in works-cited lists 36, 39, *3.3.1*
total number of volumes 51–52
museums, objects in 49–50 *See also* corporate authors
musical compositions, identified by form, number, and key 69
musical performances *See* live presentations; recordings, audio

names of persons
in fiction *1.1.3*
initials and *1.6*
*Jr.* and *Sr.* with *1.1.1, 2.1.2*
in languages other than English *1.1.4*
Asian languages 62, 63–64
French 64
German 64–65
Italian 65
Latin 65–66
romanization *1.3.8*
Spanish 66
order of *1.1.1*
pseudonymous 24, *1.1.3, 2.1.1*
roman numerals with *1.4.4, 2.1.2*
simplified *1.1.3*
in text, first and subsequent use of *1.1.1*
with titles *1.1.2*
*See also* authors' names; editors, in works-cited lists; other contributors; translators' names

names of sources *See* titles of containers; titles of sources
newspapers *See* periodicals
noun phrases, titles abbreviated as *3.2.1*
nouns
  capitalized in titles *1.2.1*
  in languages other than English *1.2.5*
novellas, titles of *1.2.2*
novels
  in containers 36
  titles of 25–27, *1.2.2*
numbers
  in in-text citations
    e-books *3.3.3*
    location indicators other than pages *3.3.2–3*, *3.6*
    paragraphs, sections, and chapters 56–57, 78, 121
    parts of poetry 121–22, *1.3.3*
    sources without page or part numbers 56
    style *3.3.1*
    works in multiple editions *3.3.2*
  in text
    beginning of sentences *1.4.1*
    commas *1.4.2*
    inclusive ranges *1.4.3*
    musical compositions 69
    paragraphs, sections, and chapters *1.6.2*
    plurals *1.4.1*
    use of numerals or words *1.4.1*
  in works-cited lists
    alphabetizing titles *2.7.4*
    discs in DVD sets 49
    editions 2.3
    episodes 40
    issues 39–40
    seasons of television series 40
numbers, in works-cited lists *(cont.)*
    versions *2.3*
    volumes 39
  *See also* page numbers; roman numerals

objects, in works-cited lists
  generic descriptions of 28–29
  locations of 49–50
online databases
  journal articles in 3
  possibly incorrect dates in 47
  in works-cited lists 31
online forums, in works-cited lists 29, 44
online usernames, of authors 24, *2.1.1*
optional elements, in works-cited lists
  access dates as 53
  cities of publication of books as 51
  dates of prior publication as 50, 53
  decisions on including 50
  series as 52
  total numbers of volumes as 51–52
  types of works as 52
organizations, romanizing non-English names of *1.3.8*
  *See also* corporate authors
other contributors 37–38
  last names of, given alone 103, *2.2.1*
  original authors as 23

page numbers
  abbreviation with *1.6.2*
  commas not used in 1.4.2
  in in-text citations 54–58, *3.3.1*
    works in multiple editions *3.3.2*

page numbers *(cont.)*
in works-cited lists
book collections 46
consecutive, in periodicals 46
not consecutive, in periodicals *2.5.1*
plus signs *2.5.1*
*See also* roman numerals
paragraph numbers *See* part numbers, other than page numbers
paragraphs
abbreviation with numbers for *1.6.2*
in block quotations 77
paraphrasing
avoiding plagiarism in 9
integrated in text *1.3.1*
sources needed for 57–58
parentheses
with quotations
alterations to sources *1.3.6*
ellipses in sources 85
real names of pseudonymous authors in *2.1.1*
in text
full Latin names 65
shortened titles *1.2.3*
translations of quotations *1.3.8*
translations of titles *1.2.5*
parenthetical documentation *See* in-text citations
Parker, William Riley x
Parks, Tim ix, xiii
part numbers, other than page numbers
abbreviations with *1.6.2*
in in-text citations 56, *3.3.2*
performances *See* film, television, and video; live presentations
periodicals
back issues of, on digital platforms 31
gathering information on 16
periodicals *(cont.)*
page numbers in, specialized style of *3.3.1*
in works-cited lists
authors 21
cities of publication of newspapers *2.6.1*
formats for titles 27–28, 30
page numbers, consecutive 46
page numbers, not consecutive *2.5.1*
pseudonymous authors 24
publication dates 42–43, 44–45
publishers omitted 42
seasons *1.5*
volume and issue numbers 39–40
*See also* articles, online and print
periods (punctuation)
in abbreviations *1.6*
ellipses with *1.3.5*
quotation marks with 88–89, *1.2.4*, *1.3.2*
in works-cited lists 20
*See also* ellipses, in quotations
permalinks 48
pinyin 63–64
place-names
in languages other than English *1.2.5*
romanizing *1.3.8*
plagiarism
avoiding 9–10
common knowledge and 10
definition of 6–7
forms of 7–9
of own writings 8
seriousness of 7
*See also* academic writing
plays *See* book collections; drama and plays
plus signs with page numbers *2.5.1*

poetry
  gathering information on 16
  quotations of *1.3.3*
    division numbers 121–22, *1.3.3*, *3.3.2*
    ellipses 83–85
    line and stanza breaks *1.3.3*
  titles of works of 26–27, *1.2.2*
    first lines as titles *1.2.1*
    titles within titles *1.2.4*
    untitled *1.2.1*
  *See also* book collections
political documents *See* corporate authors; laws, titles of; legislative bills, reports, and resolutions
*PowerPoint*, research projects presented with 128
prefaces
  documenting *2.2.1*
  referred to in text 70
prepositions in titles *1.2.1*
pronouns
  altered in quotations *1.3.1*, *1.3.6*
  capitalized in titles *1.2.1*
  in languages other than English *1.2.5*
prose style and mechanics 61–101
  abbreviations *1.6*
  dates and times *1.5*
  names of persons *1.1*
  numbers *1.4*
  quotations *1.3*
  titles of sources *1.2*
pseudonyms
  in text *1.1.3*
  in works-cited lists 24, *2.1.1*
publication dates 42–45
  gathering information on 15, 45, 46, 47
  in works-cited lists
    abbreviations for months *1.6.1*
    approximated *2.6.1*
    books 45, 46
publication dates, in works-cited lists *(cont.)*
    DVDs 44
    original 50, 53
    periodicals 45
    prior 50, 53
    television episodes 43
    Web sites 42–43, 44–45
publication facts
  evaluating 12
  gathering 13, 14–18
  missing in sources *2.6.1*
  *See also* cities of publication; copyright pages; locations; publication dates; publishers; title pages
publishers
  definition of 40
  gathering information on 14, 41, *2.4*
  in works-cited lists
    abbreviations *1.6.2–3*
    copublishers 40–41, *2.4*, *2.6.2*
    corporate authors as publishers 25, *2.1.3*
    imprints *2.4*
    missing in sources *2.6.1*
    multiple publishers of a source 40–41
    omitting publishers 42
    online media 41–42
    parent companies and divisions *2.4*
punctuation
  in abbreviations *1.6*
  in in-text citations 54–58, *3.6*
  in text
    ellipses *1.3.5*
    quotations *See* quotations
  in works-cited lists 20, *2.6*
    authors' names 21–22
    multiple works by same author *2.7.2*
    titles of containers 30
    titles of sources *1.2.1*

punctuation *(cont.)*
*See also* colons; commas; exclamation points and quotations; forward slashes; periods; question marks; quotation marks; semicolons

question marks
and quotations *1.3.7*
uncertain dates indicated by *1.5, 2.6.1*
quotation marks
in-text citations and 54
with poetry quotations *1.3.3, 1.3.7*
with prose quotations *1.3.2, 1.3.7*
single and double *1.2.4, 1.3.7–8*
with titles of sources 25–29, *1.2.2*
titles within titles and *1.2.4*
quotations *1.3*
accuracy and effective use of *1.3.1*
altered for clarity *1.3.1, 1.3.6*
block, *1.3.2–3*
of drama *1.3.4*
ellipses in *1.3.5*
in-text citations and 54–58
alterations of quotations *1.3.1, 1.3.6*
location indicators other than pages 3.3.2
of poetry *1.3.3, 1.3.7*
of prose *1.3.2, 1.3.7*
punctuation with *1.3.7*
colons before block quotations *1.3.2–3, 1.3.7*
retained from original source *1.3.7*
quotations consisting solely of *1.3.7*
titles including *1.2.1*
translations of *1.3.8*
quotations *(cont.)*
from works in multiple editions *3.3.2*
*See also* hanging indention; indention; in-text citations; quotation marks
Qur'an (Quran, Koran) 69, 122–23

recordings, audio
timings in 57
titles of songs and albums 28
versions of, in works-cited lists 39
*See also* live presentations
recordkeeping in research 8, 9–10, 12
Renaissance, names of persons in 65–66
reports *See* corporate authors; legislative bills, reports, and resolutions
*rev.* *2.3*
reviews, untitled 29 *See also* articles, online and print
romanization 63–64
of authors' names *1.3.8, 2.1.1*
of quotations 74, *1.3.8*
of titles of sources 74, *1.3.8*
*See also* languages other than English
roman numerals *1.4.4*
arabic numerals vs. *1.4*
names of persons with *1.4.4, 2.1.2*
page numbers as *3.3.1*
reduced use of xi
Roman works, ancient, documenting 122
Russian
authors' names in *2.1.1*
quotations and titles of sources in 74, *1.3.8*

*Saint*, use of title *1.1.2*
scripture
  documentation of 122–23
  titles in 69
  *See also* Bible
search engines x, 12
seasons
  in publication dates *1.5*
  of a television series 40
  *See also* dates and times
section numbers *See* part numbers, other than page numbers
self-published works 42
semicolons
  in in-text citations *1.3.8, 3.3.2, 3.6*
  with quotation marks 89
seminar titles 70
series, numbered *1.4.1* *See also* book series; film, television, and video; multivolume works
Shakespeare, William, works of
  abbreviations for titles of 100–01, *3.2.1*
  location indicators other than pages in 121–22
*sic* *1.3.6*
*Sir*, use of title *1.1.2*
slashes *See* forward slashes
slide-based presentations, research projects as 128
software
  for managing information about sources 12
  research projects presented with 128
songs *See* live presentations; recordings, audio
sources
  authority of 10–12
  differences among copies of 31
  evaluating 10–12
  gathering information on 13–18
sources *(cont.)*
  indirect 3.4
  mobility of 3
  tracking, in research 8, 9–10, 12
  *See also* books; documentation; film, television, and video; in-text citations; periodicals; quotations; titles of sources; Web sites; works-cited lists
Spanish
  names of persons in 66
  titles of sources in 74
speeches *See* live presentations
square brackets
  in in-text citations *3.6*
  with quotations
    alterations *1.3.1*
    explanations *1.3.6*
  in works-cited lists
    translations of titles *2.2.2*
    uncertain or additional information *2.6.1*
stories
  in containers 35
  titles of 26–27, *1.2.2*
  *See also* book collections
street addresses *1.4.2*
subtitles
  capitalization and punctuation of 25, 27, *1.2.1*
  finding, on books 14, 27
  omitting, in text *1.2.3*
  *See also* titles of sources
suffixes of authors' names *2.1.2*
symbols and special characters
  @ 24, *2.1.1, 2.7.1*
  accents and other diacritics *2.7.1*
  numbers used with *1.4.1*

talks *See* live presentations
Talmud
  in in-text citations 122
  title of 69

television *See* film, television, and video
*the* *See* articles (*a*, *an*, *the*)
time-based media *See* audio recordings, timings in; film, television, and video
times and time zones *1.5* *See also* dates and times
title pages
  publication dates on 45, 47
  publisher information on 14, 41, 107–09
  titles and subtitles on 26–27
titles of authors, omitted *1.1.2*, *2.1.2*
titles of containers
  definition of 30–31
  italics for *1.2.2*
  for nested containers 31–36
  *See also* book collections; book series; film, television, and video; periodicals; titles of sources; Web sites
titles of sources
  formatting *1.2*
    capitalization and punctuation *1.2.1*
    italics and quotation marks *1.2.2*
    languages other than English *1.2.5*
    quotations in titles *1.2.1*
    titles within titles *1.2.4*
    untitled poems *1.2.1*
  gathering information on 13–18, 67
  in in-text citations 55–56, *3.2*
    abbreviating titles *1.6.4*, *3.2.1*
    descriptive terms in place of titles *3.2.2*
  in text, shortened forms of *1.2.3*
  in works-cited lists 25–29, *2.2*
    alphabetizing by titles *2.7.4*
    articles online or in print 27–28
titles of sources, in works-cited lists *(cont.)*
    introductions, prefaces, forewords, and afterwords *2.2.1*
    songs and other parts of albums 28
    start of entry 24–25, *2.7.4*
    translations of titles *2.2.2*
    untitled works 28–29
  *See also* articles, online and print; blogs; books; subtitles; Web sites
*to* in infinitives in titles *1.2.1*
translations
  of quotations *1.3.8*
  of titles 72, *2.2.2*
  *See also* languages other than English; romanization
translators' names
  *my trans.* in place of *1.3.8*
  in works-cited lists 23, 37, 38
treaty titles 69
tweets, in works-cited lists
  names of authors of
    alphabetizing 112
    formatting 24
    real names added 102
  titles of 29

underlining *See* italics
uniform resource locators (URLs) 17, 48, 49, 128, *2.5.2*
United Nations, as author 25, *2.1.3*
United States, departments and agencies of, as authors *2.1.3*, *3.1.2*
United States Congress, as author 53, *2.1.3*
*University*, abbreviations of *1.6.2–3*
university presses, names of *1.6.3*
untitled sources
  poems as *1.2.1*
  in works-cited lists 28–29

Upanishads 69
URLs 17, 48, 49, 128, *2.5.2*

verbs, capitalized in titles *1.2.1*
versions
  in in-text citations
    scripture 122–23
    works in multiple editions 57, *3.3.2*
  in works-cited lists 38–39, *2.3*
video *See* film, television, and video
Vietnamese, names of persons in 63, 1.1.1
volumes *See* multivolume works
*von*, in German last names 64–65

Wade-Giles system 63–64
Web sites
  italics for titles of *1.2.2*
  in works-cited lists
    dates 42–43, 44–45, 53
    publishers 41–42
    titles 28, 30
    URLs and DOIs 17, 48, 49, 128, *2.5.2*
  *See also* articles, online and print; blogs; digital media
*Wikipedia* 12
works-cited lists 20–54, 102–16
  core elements of 20–54
    authors' names 21–25, *2.1*, *2.7.2–3*
    locations 46, 48–50
    multiple comparable items *2.6.2*
    numbers 39–40
    other contributors 37–38
    publication dates 42–45, 46, *1.5*, *1.6.1*
    publishers 40–42, *1.6.2–3*
    titles of containers 30–36

works-cited lists, core elements of *(cont.)*
    titles of sources 25–29, *1.2*, *2.2*
    versions 38–39
  cross-references in
    varying names of authors *2.1.1*
    works in collections *2.7.5*
  definition of 20
  formatting and ordering *2.7*
    hanging indention *2.7*
    heading 20, *2.7*
    letter-by-letter alphabetization *2.7.1*
    multiple works by coauthors *2.7.2–3*
    multiple works by one author *2.1.3*, *2.7.2*
    titles used for alphabetization *2.7.4*
  in-text citations in relation to 54
  names in languages other than English in *1.1.1*, *1.1.4*
  optional elements in 50–53
  organizing information for 3–4, 19
  in research projects in nonprint media 128
  seasons in *1.5*
  template for 129
  *See also* alphabetization; in-text citations; *and specific core elements for further details*
workshop titles 70

years
  approximated, in works-cited list *2.6.1*
  commas not used in *1.4.2*
  ranges of *1.4.3*
  *See also* dates and times; publication dates